PRAISE FOR *INQUIRY MINDSET*:

"Trevor MacKenzie is a gifted educator who truly puts learners at the center of his teaching. In *Inquiry Mindset: Assessment Edition*, Trevor responds to the need for a personalized, reflective, collaborative, and responsive assessment experience for all learners. Trevor's rich and reflective stories, inspiring ideas, carefully crafted processes, and guiding questions are inspiring, intentionally scaffolded, practical, and applicable to *all* age groups. With Trevor as your guide, you will find alignment to the early learning years and be left feeling empowered, supported and ready to strengthen your child-centered assessment practices."

—**Rebecca Bathurst-Hunt,** teacher and coauthor
of *Inquiry Mindset: Elementary Edition*

"This is music to my ears! Clear, personal, and eminently practical, Trevor MacKenzie's new book will be core reading for all those who, like me, believe that education has to be about building character as well as knowledge."

—**Guy Claxton,** author of *The Learning Power Approach*

"Trevor MacKenzie has done it again! He has gifted us with his heart and his mind wrapped up in a practical guide to developing more student agency in our assessment practice. At a time when many of us knew the *why* but not the *how* of inquiry, Trevor's ground-breaking books *Dive into Inquiry* and *Inquiry Mindset* gently guided us away from traditional teaching models and provided practical and engaging ways to foster student agency and develop curious, thoughtful learners. His new book, *Inquiry Mindset: Assessment Edition*, builds on the foundation of that inquiry, infusing more student voice, agency, and meaning into our assessment practice. Filled with practical tools to guide you through the behaviours, tasks, routines, and protocols, this book is the next step in developing an authentic inquiry-based classroom where students become partners in their own learning and assessment practice. A *must-have* in your classroom and schools! Thank you, Trevor!"

—**Adrienne Gear,** teacher, author, speaker

"Trevor MacKenzie is a thoughtful educator—by that I mean full of thought as well as caring and sensitive. His new book continues to share his fundamental beliefs that teaching is mostly listening and learning is mostly telling. Trevor helps his students develop and grow their capacities to become more self-assessing. He provides metacognitive prompts, reflective questions, and many processes that bring student voice into practice with a clarion call for inquiry and engagement as an integral part of evaluating their work."

—**Bena Kallick,** author of *Learning and Leading with Habits of Mind*

"Teachers committed to personalizing learning and to engaging their students in inquiry must inevitably confront an assessment question: *How do we transform a process that is typically done to students into one that honors student agency and treats them as assessment partners?* Guided by ten beliefs about student-centered assessment, this book spells out the specific steps needed to enact these beliefs. Centered by an overarching conceptual framework, MacKenzie's eminent clarity and practicality is derived from years of classroom practices. Indeed, he generously dispenses actionable nuggets on nearly every page. If you value inquiry and seek to develop reflective, self-directed students, get this book. It is brimming with advice and seasoned with soul. Your students will thank you."

—**Jay McTighe,** coauthor of the *Understanding by Design*® framework

"The Latin root of the word *assess* means "to sit beside" and that is precisely what MacKenzie does for his students and the readers of his inspiring new book. For too long, students have been left out of the assessment conversation. With stories, visuals, questions, and thoughtful examples from his own classroom, MacKenzie explains why and how we should pull up a chair for our students."

—**Kimberly Mitchell,** teacher, author of *Experience Inquiry*

"This issue of assessment is one many educators find challenging when exploring more inquiry-based approaches to teaching and learning. This book is a timely and helpful contribution to the field. Written in his characteristically warm and accessible style, Trevor has drawn largely on his own experiences as a teacher to offer solid, practical guidance, underpinned by his unwavering passion for an approach that positions the student as an empowered participant in the learning journey for which they are ultimately responsible. I have no doubt teachers will find this a valuable addition to their collection."

—**Kath Murdoch,** teacher, author of *The Power of Inquiry*

"This is the right book at the right time. Trevor's books are always chock-full of fantastic tips, tricks, and tools to help every type of educator, but this one is near and dear to my heart because assessment is the tail that wags the education dog; it's really at the heart of all learning design. Trevor outlines steps for teachers and administrators to use in designing excellent assessment for all kinds of classrooms to ensure students are truly engaged in the process—seeking feedback, using feedback to improve, and learning how to give effective feedback. I found myself earmarking almost every page with something I want to try. I work with schools around the world to help them redesign and align their curriculum and assessment, and this is a book I'll be recommending to those schools from now on. It's a perfect starting point for the work educators need to do to make assessment authentic, meaningful, and powerful."

—**Alexis Wiggins,** teacher, author of
The Best Class You Never Taught

TREVOR MACKENZIE

INQUIRY
MINDSET
ASSESSMENT EDITION

SCAFFOLDING A PARTNERSHIP FOR
EQUITY AND AGENCY IN LEARNING

Inquiry Mindset Assessment Edition
© 2021 by Trevor MacKenzie

These books are available at special discounts when purchased in quantity for use as premiums, promotions, fundraising, and educational use. For inquiries and details, contact the author: trevormackenzie.com/contact.

Published by Elevate Books EDU

Library of Congress Control Number: 2021934181
Paperback ISBN: 978-1-7352046-3-5
eBook ISBN: 978-1-7352046-4-2

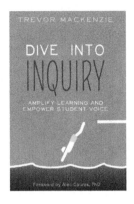

DIVE INTO INQUIRY

Amplify Learning and Empower Student Voice
By Trevor MacKenzie

Dive into Inquiry beautifully marries the voice and choice of inquiry with the structure and support required to optimize learning. With *Dive into Inquiry*, you'll gain an understanding of how to best support your learners as they shift from a traditional learning model into the inquiry classroom where student agency is fostered and celebrated each and every day.

INQUIRY MINDSET: ELEMENTARY EDITION

Nurturing the Dreams, Wonders, and Curiosities of Our Youngest Learners
By Trevor MacKenzie and Rebecca Bathurst-Hunt

Inquiry Mindset offers a highly accessible journey through inquiry in the younger years. Learn how to empower your students, increase engagement, and accelerate learning by harnessing the power of curiosity. With practical examples and a step-by-step guide to inquiry, Trevor MacKenzie and Rebecca Bathurst-Hunt make inquiry-based learning simple.

DEDICATION

THIS BOOK IS DEDICATED TO MY SONS
EWAN AND GREGOR.

THANK YOU FOR BEING UNWAVERINGLY
TRUE TO YOURSELVES IN YOUR OWN
AMAZING WAYS AND FOR CONTINUING
TO TEACH ME HOW TO BE A BETTER
VERSION OF MYSELF.

CONTENTS

SECTION 1

SECTION 2

SECTION 3

FOREWORD

Let's face it: Assessment can be vexing as a word, a concept, and a practice. Some educators fixate on it to the exclusion of good teaching practices, saying, "This is all well and good, but how do we assess it?" It's as if they see no point in creating optimal conditions for learning that engage students if, in the end, it doesn't produce an outcome that can be easily quantified. Such teachers may even prioritize assessments as the goal of teaching rather than creating optimal conditions for learning. Other times, educators get confused by the language of assessment and hence talk by, over, or past our colleagues and students because we each assume they are using the term in the same way we are. Some may use the word *assessment* to mean evaluation, grades, and scores, while others mean feedback, a conversation, or taking stock of our teaching. Even when assessment is understood to take different forms, it might be simply dichotomized as summative or formative and reduced to merely describe different types of tasks and how they get dealt with in terms of grading. And then there is the plethora of assessment practices to contend with: rubrics, portfolios, tests, conferences, exit tickets, surveys, tests, projects, and so on. To be sure, we, as a profession, need to better understand the complexities, forms, purposes, practices, goals, and meanings of assessment. What might it look like to map the broad terrain of assessment?

I propose that we think of assessment as occurring on two dimensions. The first dimension (let's set this on a horizontal continua), is the degree of evaluation in which we engage. At the far end of this continua (we'll place it on the right), we are highly evaluative, desiring scores and measures that quantify outcomes in a fairly precise way. Here, we judge work against clearly defined criteria that we apply to see just how close to the mark a student gets. Such evaluation can produce ranks and comparisons. On the other end of this continua (we'll place it on the left), we might seek to understand students where they are, making sense of their actions and responding through our grounded interpretation. Here, rather than coming with predetermined criteria, we open ourselves to the possibilities and variations in both learning styles and outcomes that a close examination of our students' learning might provide.

The second dimension (let's set this on a vertical continua), is the extent to which our assessments are integrated in our instruction and are part of the ongoing learning of the classroom. At one end (we'll place it at the top), we have assessment that is highly embedded in our teaching and students' learning. That means that we don't stop or pause our instruction in order to assess but instead embed it as a regular part of our practice. At the other end of the continua (placed at the bottom), we have assessment that is set apart from instruction and student learning. Here, we declare a formal end to our instruction and move into a deliberate assessment phase that we hope will reveal something about students' learning.

A basic graph of these two dimensions produces four quadrants that we might use to map the terrain of assessment. (See Figure 1.)

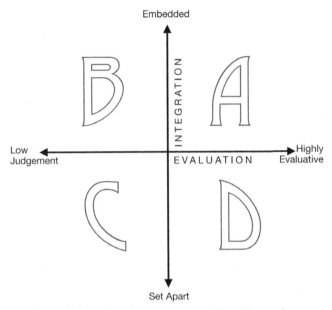

Figure 1: Mapping Assessment on Two Dimensions

With this map of the terrain in hand, we can begin to place our various assessment practices in the appropriate quadrant. Let's begin with Quadrant D since this represents the traditional way schools have thought about assessment. This quadrant is characterized by highly evaluative practices that are set apart from our teaching practice: *The teaching is completed, and now it is time for students to show their learning in a manner we can evaluate.* Here we have practices such as tests and formal summative assessments. In the farthest extreme of the lower, right-hand corner we have district, state, or provincial tests, national exams, or tests administered by outside agencies.

Continuing in the "set apart" range, let's consider the assessment practices of Quadrant C. These practices once again are characterized as not an embedded part of our teaching, but they differ from Quadrant D in that they are "low judgement" and more interpretive in nature. Examples here would be the practice of "Looking at Student Work" (LASW), examination of teacher's documentation of learning, or video analysis. Typically these practices are done as part of a professional learning group and aided by the use of protocols. The goal here is not to evaluate students or score their work, but to look for learning in whatever form it might take. Another assessment practice that fits in this quadrant is clinical interviewing in which we remove students from class to engage in one-on-one interviews to help us learn more about students' learning. Such interviews can be evaluative, if one has in mind a ranking or comparison of students, or interpretative, such as Piagetian-style interviews.

Moving to the upper part of our map, let us consider Quadrant B. Here we have assessment that is low in its judgment and embedded in our instruction. This is the assessment that happens in class and informs our instruction on the spot. We might call this kind of assessment part of our *formative and responsive practice* as teachers. We read the class, we gather clues and evidence, we check for understanding and misconceptions all with an eye toward modifying our instruction. This is perhaps one of the key skills teachers acquire over time and one that beginning teachers strive to master. One way to help develop these skills is by spending time engaging in Quadrant B practices. When we look carefully at documentation of learning in a low-stress, set-apart context, we begin to develop the eyes with which to see learning as it unfolds in front of us.

Finally, we arrive at Quadrant A, in which our assessment practices are embedded in our teaching and students' learning and are evaluative in nature. To be evaluative should not be considered negatively. One wants their swim coach to evaluate one's stroke and consistency, for instance. Building class criteria of what quality work looks like can be extremely useful. Nor does evaluation always have to come from the outside. As a learner, one can set goals for oneself that can be used to evaluate progress. One practice in this quadrant is the feedback we provide to students on their performance. To give effective feedback, some criteria has to be applied. Providing good feedback on students' writing requires that we understand what constitutes quality writing, how far the student is from that goal, and what immediate actions might allow them to make some progress. The use of rubrics or success criteria as well as student and peer assessment practices also fit in this quadrant.

The point of this mapping is not to label any of these sets of practices as good or bad but to map the terrain, to provide a bird's eye view, if you will, about what assessment can mean in different contexts. All of these assessment practices have their place and purpose. Another point of a map is to help us navigate—to know where we are, and where we might go or want to be. Where do your current assessment practices fit on the map? Are you and your colleagues spending most of your time in Quadrant D as many teachers do? What other quadrants need to be explored?

As you read, Trevor MacKenzie's *Inquiry Mindset: Assessment Edition*, I hope this orientation will be helpful as you both navigate and explore the rich and varied terrain of assessment he lays out for us as readers. As he shares various practices with you, think about where they might fit on the map. How embedded are they? How much evaluation is going on? As you read, you'll find that Trevor takes us deep inside the practices associated with Quadrant A, providing real, classroom examples that help us better understand what is possible in this area. Most importantly perhaps, he shows us what is possible to do with our students as co-collaborators. He helps us explore the forms assessment practices in this quadrant can take when we adopt the mindset of assessment as something we do with our students rather than do to them.

Trevor also invites us into the deep, rich, and sometimes challenging practices of Quadrant B. These assessment skills, what I have called *formative and responsive practices*, can be hard to acquire and, at times, challenging to fully understand. While this is true for new teachers, it is also true for anyone just starting their journey as an inquiry teacher. As Trevor himself mentions, "I've come to understand that one of the most powerful behaviours exhibited by a teacher in inquiry is their responsiveness." He calls this the "power of the pivot," and invites us into his thinking as a master facilitator of student inquiry and experienced coach. When an expert makes their thinking visible to us, as Trevor does here, we are invited into a cognitive apprenticeship in which we not only learn the expert's practices but also the expert's way of thinking.

Quadrant C and D are not neglected. Trevor discusses how to bring students into reporting practices, which, by their nature, are summative. He also discusses the importance of learning from and with our colleagues as we discuss student learning, articulate and share our values, and collaboratively analyze student learning.

With a new map in hand and Trevor's practical experience and wisdom laid out before you, I send you off to enjoy your journey!

RON RITCHHART

Harvard Graduate School of Education
Cambridge, Massachusetts

INTRODUCTION

I haven't always been an inquiry teacher.

I didn't experience an inquiry model as a child. My formal education was not, in any way that I can recall, built on the constructivist values I now hold dear. My teacher training, although at a fantastic university with committed and informed professors, didn't introduce me to this broad and rich school of thinking that has become part of who I am; in fact, I didn't learn the beautiful language of inquiry until I was well into my career.

I became an inquiry teacher because of my students. Essentially, *my students taught me how to teach.*

After several years of trying to meet the needs of my students, slowly, over time, I asked them more questions about themselves. I asked them about their interests and hobbies and curiosities. I asked them about their dreams and their goals and their wishes for themselves. I asked them about their learning and their strengths and their stretches.

I asked, and then I *listened* to what they had to say, and ultimately, I learned from them.

A magical thing happened: The more I listened and learned and allowed what they told me to direct my teaching, the more I realized I was changing. I was becoming a different teacher. In learning about my students, I discovered things about myself, about my practice, and about my profession.

I started letting my teaching touch my heart and guide my actions.

I discovered a gentleness in teaching, a soft spot in the tensions and challenges of our practice. I found an ebb and flow—an ease—that offered me an opportunity to settle into myself and, in turn, to give my students the opportunity to settle into themselves.

I unearthed a partnership that felt natural, organic, and symbiotic. Our classroom felt more like an ecosystem, a natural space where everything had its place and purpose and was integral to each thing and being. I realized that we were all a part of something bigger than ourselves.

When it came to my teaching and my time in my school, I slowly started to care about absolutely everything in a very seamless and easy way. I noticed all the small occurrences in learning. I observed how even the slightest of shifts could have lasting effects. I discovered a powerful value in particular moves, behaviours, questions, and dispositions.

It felt as though I was discovering a secret language that I had always known existed but had never heard spoken aloud before.

Now, so many years later, I still allow my students to guide me. I still lean into questions and let them shape my learning and my growth. Just as I did when I first took steps toward becoming an inquiry teacher, I continue to allow questions to direct my journey.

One specific question comes to mind as I reflect on the course of my learning and our next steps together in the book before you. It's a question that guides most of the decisions I make in my inquiry practice. It shapes my unit design, my planning, and my lesson preparation. I reflect on this question countless times in a single day. It is always present.

Am I doing something for my students that they should be doing for themselves?

Exploring this question in my inquiry practice allows me to consider who is doing the heavy lifting of learning, who is benefiting from the decision-making in the classroom, and who is sharpening the skills, competencies, and mindsets to take on more agency over learning. Time and time again, when I ponder this question, I realize that there is so much more I can be facilitating for my students to have them take on more ownership of their learning. I have come to realize that I have been trained, conditioned even, to hold the reins of learning in the classroom too tightly, too closely, and too guardedly. I recognize, however, that for inquiry to take hold in the classroom and in my students' hearts and minds, I need to loosen those reins and give my students the freedom to take the lead.

I have been asking teachers in schools around the world the same question as I support them in implementing inquiry values and practices. In guiding teachers toward embedding more student agency in their classrooms, this guiding question shapes our reflections, discussions, and planning. These collaborations provide powerful opportunities to push practice forward, to work toward something larger than ourselves, and to connect and work together to create lifelong learners, global citizens, and empathetic humanitarians.

I've consistently noticed one realm within our inquiry practice where exploring this question tends to stall—one area that has been slower to shift and reimagine. In this one facet of teaching and learning, student agency doesn't blossom as fruitfully or flow as fluidly as it does in others. This was the most difficult shift for me to make in my inquiry practice, and it tends to be the last shift I observe in the schools I support in inquiry. It is in the realm of assessment.

I have noticed several things in my work that suggest this is true.

First, assessment tends to be something mostly done outside of the classroom, *away* from students, rather than inside the classroom *with* the students. If those who are doing the assessing are doing the learning, why are teachers working harder than students?

Second, teachers have a strong understanding of where students are, where they need to go next, and what they need to do to get there, but students don't. If I were to confer with students in learning and ask them to share with me their next steps, many students would not be able to participate in that conversation. Why is this the case?

Third, students have little understanding of success criteria, assessment tools, or learning objectives and goals. Why isn't there transparency regarding what students will be assessed on and how they will be assessed?

Fourth, there are frequent opportunities to reflect and confer in the experience of inquiry but not in the assessments in inquiry. Why does a misalignment exist here?

Finally, students share feelings of confidence, ownership, and fulfillment regarding inquiry, but when it comes to assessment, they feel anxious, overwhelmed, and uncertain. Why the difference?

This book aims to nurture more student voice, involvement, and agency in the assessment realm of inquiry so these challenges don't occur. For this to be achieved, teachers need to help students fine-tune their assessment compass—their ability to assess with accuracy, clarity, fulfillment, and authenticity. This book is rooted in the values of inquiry. It will guide you through the behaviours, tasks, routines, and protocols that will help nurture the mindset of agency and cultivate accurate and confident assessment experts in your classroom.

With this in mind, I propose you keep three big ideas in mind as you read this book. These three big ideas will act as guiding principles as you transition into including more student agency in your assessment practice:

1. **Let's break down the comparison culture of assessment.**

   Throughout their education, our students have encountered particular experiences with assessment that have had a lasting negative impact on how they respond to learning and, more detrimentally, how they see themselves as learners. We need to move away from an assessment practice that reinforces comparison and toward an assessment practice that supports self-reflection, individual growth, and personal achievement. We need to have students reconnect with an overarching truth in learning: that your growth isn't measured against someone else's growth; your growth is measured by reflecting on where you were before and how far you've come across time.

   I propose we shed light on this truth *with* our students so that we can begin to move toward an inquiry and assessment space that is much more meaningful to each and every learner in our classrooms. As you'll experience in these pages, many powerful activities can help students redefine success in school to focus on personal growth and fulfillment. Our job is to wade into this transition slowly, scaffolding when needed and gradually shifting control over assessment from the teacher to the learner as a shared partnership in inquiry.

2. **Let's infuse more student voice in assessment.**

   By the end of this book, you will be ready to co-design assessment *with your students*. Every learning objective, every prescribed outcome, every mandated assessment tool, and every rubric and criteria used in your classroom could be infused with student voice. Your learners will have a direct hand in the assessment frameworks you use. The benefits of student voice in assessment include a greater understanding of how to succeed in class, the potential for increased achievement for your students, and a more meaningful and fulfilling student experience in our schools. It all begins with student voice and giving our learners a seat at the table of assessment.

3. **Let's be brave in letting go of some of our beliefs around teaching and learning.**

   You may recognize some of what I propose, and thus it may feel comfortable and reaffirming as you read. You may very well see yourself in the values, beliefs, activities, and frameworks outlined in this book. Some of what I share, however, may raise feelings of uncertainty. You may feel a particular tension in sharing a role with your students regarding assessment in your classroom. Please consider this: It is in this uncertainty and tension that great things will happen for your students. As they become more willing and competent assessors themselves, the student agency experienced will have a lasting positive impact for years to come. When students can self-assess with confidence and accuracy, they are sharpening tools they will use throughout their lives. They will become reflective, process focused, self-motivated, and active participants in their schooling experience. Big things await when you get comfortable in the mess of uncertainty. I encourage you to be brave and take some small steps toward making these big changes a reality for you and your students.

   I now invite you to inquire into your inquiry practice. Grab a notebook to document your reflections, and let's settle into this learning together.

   Enjoy!

   Trevor

HOW TO USE
#INQUIRYMINDSET IN ACTION

At the end of each chapter of *Inquiry Mindset*, you'll discover prompts I have termed #InquiryMindset in Action. These short and powerful calls to action will ask you to reflect on your reading and put some of what I propose into action. Once you've done so, I ask that you capture and share these actions items with the #InquiryMindset community by tweeting them out, sharing them with your Instagram friends, and posting them in your Facebook groups. In inquiry, we are all better together. With this in mind, let's all commit to sharing our learning as we read so we can collectively support one another in becoming the teachers our students need. Please have a notebook at the ready to help document and reflect throughout your reading. Enjoy!

 In inquiry, we are all better together.

GET EVEN MORE FROM *INQUIRY MINDSET:*
ASSESSMENT EDITION ONLINE!

Download Inquiry Mindset sketchnotes and book club resources as well a companion guide for primary teachers at **trevormackenzie.com/companionresources**.

SECTION 1

STUDENT-CENTRED ASSESSMENT BELIEFS

Over the course of my journey into inquiry, I have witnessed the many benefits of co-designing and co-constructing with students. When it comes to assessment, this sort of partnership in learning has incredibly powerful and lasting effects. I have had experiences in both realities: a co-designed inquiry approach to learning as well as a teacher-controlled, prescriptive, and standardized approach to assessment.

In one reality, I am able ensure that there is a rich connection between student learning and assessment. This connection provides a sense of belonging and control over assessment for the student. It creates clarity and confidence over assessment whilst slowly yet positively impacting achievement in the student's schooling.

In the other reality, a previous version of my current inquiry-self, I acted as the lone assessment expert in the classroom. Although I had a clear understanding of the assessment realm of learning, this space was completely void of student voice, engagement, and understanding.

A recent experience highlighted for me the difference in these two realities—and how much has changed for me and, more importantly, for my students. While conferring with a small group of students about their learning, I asked them a few guiding questions, prompting them to reflect on their learning. I requested that they identify areas of their learning that they were proud of, share specific things they would like to improve on, and collaboratively provide feedback on one another's reflections. As I asked this group of students to begin, they confidently took the lead in their learning. Their reflections were powerfully robust, clear, and intentional. Their insights into one another's learning were kind yet helpful. It was respectful yet *growth focused*. Their feedback pushed each other to improve, yet it was full of empathy and understanding for one another.

It was one of those teacher moments where I just could not believe what I was witnessing. The experience struck me as being a successful culmination of particular beliefs and values that have helped shape what assessment and inquiry look like in my classroom.

Through co-designing learning and finding an authentic partnership with your students, you'll be making an investment in your students that goes far beyond the classroom and the curriculum. You'll be investing in agency over learning, the competencies and dispositions that will transcend their schooling, and the mindsets that will provide students with a foundation in life to discover fulfillment, meaning, and success in their future endeavours.

The behaviours, tasks, routines, and protocols proposed throughout this book will call on you to make changes to how you spend time with students, how you plan what learning looks like in the classroom, and how you engage with students about their learning. In reality, none of benefits I've listed can be achieved unless we prioritize and weave the behaviours, tasks, routines, and protocols proposed throughout this book into our daily practice. If we don't embody the values that underpin such a reimagining of assessment in inquiry, this vital area of our practice will remain stalled and largely ineffective.

> Through co-designing learning and finding an authentic partnership with your students, you're investing in student fulfillment, meaning, and success in their future endeavours.

These values are reflected in the Student-Centred Assessment Beliefs, which set the stage for teachers to give students a seat at the table of assessment. It is in these values that teachers will discover the time, space, and commitment to provide more agency over the assessment realm of inquiry. It is in these values that faculties and teams of teachers will leverage collaboration to create assessment alignment, capacity, and a culture of inquiry. It is in these values that schools will begin to help raise the threshold of student achievement, fulfillment, and belonging.

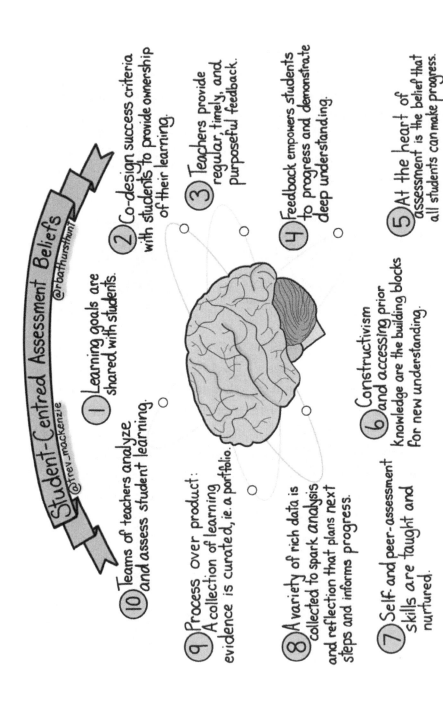

Student-Centred Assessment Beliefs

@trev_mackenzie   @reathursthunt

1. Learning goals are shared with students.

2. Co-design success criteria with students to provide ownership of their learning.

3. Teachers provide regular, timely, and purposeful feedback.

4. Feedback empowers students to progress and demonstrate deep understanding.

5. At the heart of assessment is the belief that all students can make progress.

6. Constructivism and accessing prior knowledge are the building blocks for new understanding.

7. Self- and peer-assessment skills are taught and nurtured.

8. A variety of rich data is collected to spark analysis and reflection that plans next steps and informs progress.

9. Process over product: A collection of learning evidence is curated, ie. a portfolio.

10. Teams of teachers analyze and assess student learning.

Created in collaboration with IS Basel, Switzerland

#InquiryMindset

As you explore the Student-Centred Assessment Beliefs, reflect on the following:

- Do any of these values currently align with the culture of inquiry in your classroom and the decisions you make around how you spend time with your students?
- If you find alignment, what does this look like in practice? How does each specific value currently surface in the behaviours, tasks, routines, and protocols that come together to form the culture of inquiry in your classroom?
- In which values could you bring more intentionality, consistency, and growth in your practice? If you were asked to select a Student-Centred Assessment Beliefs goal, something that you will work toward implementing more holistically in your teaching, what would your goal be?

Let's take a closer look at the Student-Centred Assessment Beliefs and how classrooms that hold to these beliefs operate:

1. Learning goals are shared with students.

The objectives and standards of the curriculum are actively discussed and referred to throughout the learning process. These learning goals can be visibly displayed in the classroom, as they can anchor student goal setting, planning, and reflection. Learning goals are not understood by the teacher alone; rather, every student can articulate what he or she is learning toward, how they (both collectively with the teacher and other students and individually) are planning on getting there, and how assessment will play a role in this process. Learning goals are not hidden. Neither is there a Wizard of Oz effect in place, in which the teacher omnisciently orchestrates the learning toward the goals without any knowledge of them by the students. Every stakeholder in the learning community knows the learning goals.

2. **Co-design success criteria with students to provide ownership over learning.**

   Any success criteria, whether mandated and standardized or designed organically with students, is co-designed *with* students. Teachers facilitate discourse. They unpack and make sure students have a clear understanding of the success criteria through collaborative and co-designed protocols. In this co-design process, students become more knowledgeable of what success in learning should look like. They also have a direct, powerful, and authentic voice to help shape the success criteria.

3. **Teachers provide regular, timely, and purposeful feedback.**

   Regular means that feedback is consistent, routinized, and a part of the culture of inquiry in the classroom. *Feedback* happens all the time. It is a consistent and nonthreatening part of the learning experience. *Timely* means in the learning and not after class, in isolation, or absent of students. Timely feedback occurs when it will stick and when students can immediately demonstrate they understand the feedback because they can take it and apply it to their learning. *Purposeful* means that the feedback will drive the next steps in clear ways that students understand. Purposeful means feedback is in scaffolded steps and student-friendly language.

4. **Feedback empowers students to progress and demonstrate deep understanding.**

   Students have time, space, and support to take the feedback and progress. Class time is devoted to the rich process of having students use feedback to demonstrate progress. Feedback elevates learning, sharpens thinking, shapes competencies, and leads to deep understanding. Feedback supports growth over time and not merely growth in tasks or assignments. Feedback is collaborative in the classroom. Over time, students become competent peer and self-assessors as they learn to give accurate and purposeful feedback to empower one another.

5. **At the heart of assessment is the belief that all students can make progress.**

All students are capable of success in class. All students possess strengths that allow them to enter learning and assessment with confidence and a strong sense of self, autonomy, and ownership. Teachers lift up students' strengths and provide opportunities for them to be leveraged in learning. Conversely, all students possess stretches, areas that could be barriers to success. In a classroom with a culture of inquiry, the students and teacher work together to support everyone's learning so each person makes progress and grows.

6. **Constructivism and accessing prior knowledge are the building blocks for new understanding.**

Students enter the classroom with rich experiences, narratives, values, beliefs, and prior knowledge. Teachers actively seek out ways to get to know their students—who they are and what they know. This process occurs constantly in the classroom. Teachers and students access this prior knowledge and leverage it. In doing so, they make the curriculum and assessment responsive to their students and take advantage of what they bring to the learning each and every day.

7. **Self- and peer-assessment skills are taught and nurtured.**

Self- and peer-assessment skills are actively and consistently coached, modeled. and scaffolded. Teachers clearly communicate these skills and may visibly display them in the classroom to help drive reflection, feedback, and planning. Students are encouraged to self-assess through guiding questions, thinking routines, and collaborative talk structures. Teachers aim to fine-tune students' assessment compass for accuracy, clarity, fulfillment, and authenticity. Students need to feel psychologically safe to give, accept, and use feedback that will propel learning.

8. **A variety of rich data are collected to spark analysis and reflection that support planning next steps and inform progress.**

Evidence is varied, diverse, and somewhat responsive to the students in the classroom based on the strengths and stretches students bring to learning. Some assignments, tasks, and routines will be teacher directed. Some assignments, tasks, and routines will be student centered and selected. All learners are given the time, space, and support to make meaning of the data, to discuss them with the teacher and their peers, to pick them apart, and to plan next steps.

9. **Process over product: A collection of learning evidence is curated.**

Teachers aim to find a balance between learning and performing, and between formative and summative assessments. If we have an assessment culture of too many performances and summative assessments, we run the risk of creating an assessment culture of comparison and hoop jumping. For some students, this causes feelings of anxiety, stress, and of being overwhelmed.

Embedding more opportunities to get feedback and apply it to the learning and growth of each individual student allows students to settle into the process of learning as opposed to merely going through the motions of the performance of learning. Over time, students curate a vibrant range of evidence that they and their teachers can analyze and reflect on to plan next steps.

10. Teams of teachers analyze and assess learning.

Teachers have the time to come together as faculties or teams to analyze and assess learning. Teachers actively and openly share the behaviours, tasks, routines, and protocols that create more agency over assessment in their classrooms. Teachers themselves fine-tune their assessment compasses as they discover alignment and capacity within their faculties and teams. Students experience assessment equity as teachers actively and openly share and collaborate. Time is a key factor here. Teachers spend time together conferring and analyzing.

The Student-Centred Assessment Beliefs directly shape the behaviours, tasks, routines, and protocols proposed throughout this book. Essentially the chapters that follow are the implementational side of these values. They reveal what each belief looks like in practice with teachers and students as partners in inquiry. Your reflection on the Student-Centred Assessment Beliefs, the alignment you discovered, and your active commitment to bringing more intentionality to the areas you have decided to work toward will create a personalized journey through this book. Although I am certain you'll find that each chapter elevates your inquiry practice, it's the areas of intentional focus and goalsetting that will likely reap the greatest rewards for you individually. Keep this in mind as you embark on your reading of each chapter.

#INQUIRYMINDSET IN ACTION

In this chapter, I asked you to reflect on the following prompts regarding the Student-Centred Assessment Beliefs:

- Do any of these values currently align with the culture of inquiry in your classroom and the decisions you make around how you spend time with your students?
- If you find alignment, what does this look like in practice? How does each specific value currently surface in the behaviours, tasks, routines, and protocols that together form the culture of inquiry in your classroom?
- In which values could you bring more intentionality, consistency, and growth in your practice? If you were asked to select a Student-Centred Assessment Beliefs goal, something that you will work toward implementing more holistically in your teaching, what would your goal be?

Please record your reflections now and highlight the specific goal or goals you have set for yourself.

NURTURE STUDENT OWNERSHIP OF ASSESSMENT

My student and I stood in the hallway just outside of my classroom, reviewing a series of artifacts she had created as part of her demonstration of understanding. As we chatted about her learning, I recognized the power and value of this culminating conversation. I had worked with this student for three years. During that time, I had learned several things about her, including the reasons that made it incredibly challenging for her to take ownership over her learning and voice in assessment.

She had shared with me that she was full of self-doubt and that she always, *always*, undervalued her capabilities.

She had shared with me that there seemed to be a little voice inside of her that told her she wasn't good enough and that no matter how hard she tried, she would never be good enough.

She had shared with me that my coaching and scaffolding caused a genuine fear and anxiety about taking on what I was proposing.

Agency and ownership frightened her. Agency and ownership felt overwhelming, debilitating, and scary.

Despite her lack of confidence and at times crippling anxiety, there we were, standing together talking about her body of work. Not only could I see how much she had learned, but I could also see how much she had gained. She stood tall, shoulders back. Her concise and passionate words related her insightful and personal reflections.

In that moment, my student embodied the benefits of small steps taken over time—steps I had taken to scaffold inquiry and agency of both learning and assessment. All of those small steps, all of the words of encouragement and support, all of the small shifts toward empowerment had helped her discover a positive outlook on her learning and a genuine self-worth she hadn't felt before.

In my inquiry experiences working with students in the classroom and with teachers in schools around the world, I have observed that student agency is more likely to be successfully achieved if strong and clear scaffolding is identified and planned. As we communicate the vision and outline the small steps we will take to make this new vision a reality, a clear scaffolding takes shape, and a direction and process emerge. With planning, intentionality, implementation, reflection, revision, and responsiveness, the small steps toward the reimagined landscape eventually yield the benefits of a learning experience that is rich in student agency.

This is how inquiry thrives. Not by throwing our kids into the deep end of the inquiry pool or by backing away from learning entirely. Inquiry thrives as we become partners in learning. Inquiry thrives when it is coached and modeled. Inquiry thrives when we scaffold for the understanding and acquisition of the skills of agency.

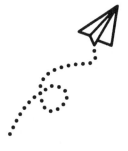

Inquiry thrives as we become partners in learning.

Inquiry thrives when it is coached and modeled.

Inquiry thrives when we scaffold for the understanding and acquisition of the skills of agency.

If we want our students to be more meaningfully involved in the assessment of their learning, we must scaffold and take small steps toward a reimagined assessment experience. We must provide the structure that equips students to engage in reflective practice and thinking and empowers them to do more of the heavy lifting of assessment. To that end, I've identified ten small steps you can take to support your students as they take ownership of their assessment.

The 10 Steps to Nurture Student Ownership of Assessment is a conceptual framework that provides the necessary scaffolding. This series of behaviours, tasks, routines, and protocols, when woven together over time, create an assessment continuum that fine-tunes our students' assessment compass.

Here's how the 10 Steps to Nurture Student Ownership of Assessment play out in the inquiry classroom:

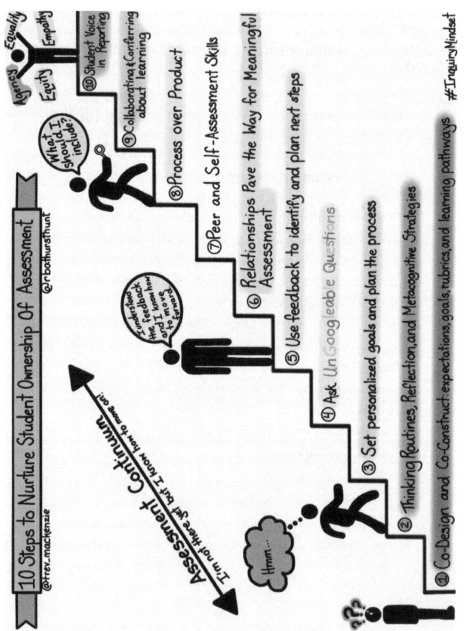

1. **Co-Design and Co-Construct**

   This process of co-designing underpins the inquiry model and builds a culture of togetherness where the teacher and the student are partners in learning and partners in assessment. In the inquiry classroom, students take on the heavy lifting of assessment.

2. **Thinking Routines, Reflection, and Metacognitive Strategies**

   Reflection and student-led discussion play an important role in creating agency of assessment and in guiding learning. At the same time, hearing from students informs teacher practice.

3. **Set Personalized Goals and Plan the Process**

   Some of the assessment load will be shaped by the students' personal learning goals. With their goals in mind, they can plan next steps and curate evidence to track growth. Having goals also helps shape their reflective practice and informs the connections they make to themselves, the curriculum, and the world.

4. **Ask UnGoogleable Questions**

   The role of questions is to shape learning and conceptual understanding. Questions should guide reflection and direct the learning process. Use open-ended, thought-provoking, unGoogleable questions to make thinking and learning visible.

5. **Use Feedback to Identify and Plan Next Steps**

   Authentic learning and growth require risk-taking. Vulnerability, safety, and trust are essential to creating an environment where students feel confident accepting and giving feedback that helps guide next steps.

6. Relationships Pave the Way for Meaningful Assessment
Strong bonds between the teacher and each student as well as amongst the students build trust over time. This trust is the foundation for students feeling safe to take risks in their learning, to give and receive feedback without fear of ridicule or persecution, and to become more confident in taking on more agency over learning.

7. Peer and Self-Assessment
For these to occur with accuracy and clarity whilst being helpful and authentic to the recipient, strong relationships must be nurtured by everyone in the learning community.

8. Process over Product
Traditional classrooms focus on performance. Inquiry classrooms make sure that the learning process takes precedence and students are empowered to take on more agency over their assessment.

9. Collaborating and Conferring about Learning
Create natural and consistent opportunities for teachers and students to talk about learning, track growth and progress, identify next steps, and learn how to differentiate and revise the learning steps.

10. Student Voice in Reporting
The culmination of this scaffolding creates the foundation for the teacher and student to co-construct report cards and other avenues for formal assessment communication.

NEXT STEPS

In the next several chapters, we will look at each step in much more detail. As you progress through the steps, you'll find ideas to guide your planning and shape the reimagining of your inquiry practice. My hope is that you will bring these ideas to your students in the classroom and use them to slowly and intentionally reshape the landscape of assessment with your learners. As you put these ideas into action, your students will become more proficient, accurate, and confident in their role in assessment.

Let's dive in!

#INQUIRYMINDSET IN ACTION

In reflecting on the 10 Steps to Nurture Student Ownership of Assessment, are there any steps that stand out to you—an area in which you have some experience, competency, or expertise? Conversely, in which of the 10 Steps to Nurture Student Ownership of Assessment do you feel you have less experience, competency, or expertise? Document these areas and be prepared for a close reading of the chapters focused on those areas.

SECTION 2

CO–DESIGN AND
CO–CONSTRUCT

Co-designing learning with students and involving their voice in the learning process in a variety of ways is essential to the inquiry model. Student choice is part of co-designing, but it is only one aspect of what it means to construct learning *with* students. A choice, for example, in how to demonstrate learning is an important facet of student agency because it provides students with a strength-based start point in learning rather than a deficit one. But without the other facets of student agency, this choice simply won't do. Student agency is about so much more than providing a menu of options; it is about empowering learners.

The benefits of co-designing learning with students are numerous:

1. **Students see that their voice matters in an authentic manner.** They see that learning is a partnership between student and teacher and that their decisions hold weight in the classroom. They learn to reflect on their strengths and

stretches. They share their curiosities and wonderings more openly in the classroom. They become more active and take on more responsibility in their learning.

2. **Teachers can more powerfully meet the needs of their diverse classrooms by planning learning with students rather than for students.** As we get to know our students, we can create structures and pathways that empower them in their learning. We can be more responsive to our students' needs. The growing child is seeking autonomy and agency. By co-designing learning with students, teachers can coach, model, and differentiate to best support students in taking on the heavy lifting in learning.

3. **The learning community is shaped by teachers and students working together.** No longer is schooling a top-down experience in which complacency, passivity, and disengagement are all too often the student experience. Students see their self-worth as being more than a score. Students recognize that they are part of something bigger than themselves: a community that plans together, works together, and grows together. Teachers, too, see themselves as part of a community in which they experience a shared ownership over learning. As teachers empower students in this heavy lifting of learning, two amazing benefits occur: students gain more agency over learning, and teachers discover a balance in their workload.

This all occurs over time, as an accumulation of events, talks, experiences, and relationships within the classroom. No one discussion, no single student conference, and no isolated experience or event will create the genuine student agency or learning community outlined above. It is with consistent scaffolding, clear values, and a continual connection to co-designing that students become increasingly successful in taking ownership over their learning.

> Inquiry nurtures a schooling experience that is no longer a top-down experience for students in which complacency, passivity, and disengagement are all too often the norm.

You can intentionally plan for and implement co-designing opportunities that will help create the landscape for student agency, and it begins by establishing a partnership on the first day of school. Your initial steps into sharing the heavy lifting of learning with your students are so important in helping them to understand that this learning experience will be a different one than they have experienced before, one in which they are active participants in the decision-making of learning. Consider beginning to share this heavy lifting with your students as soon as you meet them, in your first interaction with them.

EXPECTATIONS AND ROUTINES

In my experience, teachers who outline classroom expectations and routines *with students* rather than *for students* get much more traction when it comes to building the kind of learning community they desire. By posing a series of guiding questions, getting students talking and sharing ideas in small groups, and gathering information to synthesize and draw conclusions from, teachers can start the process of co-designing the type of classroom where agency will thrive.

Here are some guiding questions I enjoy using to help this discussion flourish:

- What does great learning mean to you?
- How do you know you are ready to learn?
- What do you need from your teacher, from your peers, and from yourself to be ready for learning?
- What does great collaboration look like?
- What words describe a learning community?
- How should we take turns sharing ideas?
- How can we be respectful in hearing and understanding one another?
- How can we transition smoothly throughout our time together so everyone can find balance and ease in their learning?

It is important to synthesize and make connections with all that surfaces from these guiding questions. I suggest recording all ideas from the small groups into a common space such as on your whiteboard or a Google Doc or a Padlet. As ideas emerge and the sharing becomes more abundant, try to cluster ideas by categorizing similar answers, finding commonalities and synonyms to create clarity and unity. By actively and intentionally making connections, students learn how to move from independent responses to a unified, co-designed landscape.

Once the thinking has been synthesized, it is important to make these clustered ideas visible in the classroom so that the co-designed document becomes a collective commitment to recognized beliefs and practices. Make it visible, and then you can refer to it throughout the year with students as learning is occurring. When the opportunity arises, pause and talk about the points that surfaced in your initial conversation. If the circumstances during which you co-designed these expectations and routines have changed, take the time to revise your document. The conversation, although solidified in this doc, is ongoing. Our learners grow and change throughout the year; so should this doc.

COMPETENCIES AND DISPOSITIONS

The skill set students require to be successful in taking on more agency over learning in the classroom setting is powerfully akin to the skills today's employers are looking for when they hire. Do a simple Google search of "the skills you need to succeed," and you'll see similarities outlined in current articles from a plethora of magazines, newspapers, and research houses.

How do you prepare students to grapple with and solve the problems of tomorrow in the classrooms of today? I propose that inquiry is the process by which this can be accomplished. The competencies and dispositions inquiry encourages are critical in ensuring students can be successful in taking on a more meaningful role in their learning and more responsibility as a productive citizen as they mature.

Competencies, dispositions, and habits of mind are the foundation for rich, authentic, and successful student agency.

With this being the case, I don't merely give my students a list of competencies and dispositions that we will work with throughout our time together. No. Rather I co-design this list of competencies and dispositions with them.

I start by asking my students to define competencies and dispositions, and how they are important for learning. If students do not know what these important words mean, we do some research. As we share our ideas and findings, the words take shape in our classroom.

I then ask students what competencies and dispositions are important in today's workplace and skills they think they will need to succeed in 2021 and beyond. In small groups, students discuss these prompts and even do a bit of research. From their findings and conversations, we create a list of competencies and dispositions in a common space (whiteboard or Google Doc or Padlet). I synthesize their ideas, modeling what I notice and observe so they can begin to take on this decision-making process on their own at some point in our time together; for example, a recent class identified seven competencies and dispositions that we agreed to reflect on and work toward sharpening individually and collectively:

1. Critical thinking
2. Collaboration
3. Communication
4. Creativity
5. Empathy
6. Self-Control
7. Curiosity

We created large posters for each competency that students illustrated. We then displayed these in our classroom to use as visual reflection prompts and talking points throughout the year. These helped me pause the learning and point out to students when I noticed that these rich skills and mindsets were at work. I would call a "learning time-out" so I could connect what students were engaged in with the topic of one of the posters they had created and collaboratively agreed on working toward.

Furthermore, students and I co-designed specific written reflection prompts as to what each competency looked like and *sounded* like. We printed each of these off and displayed them beside the posters so students could make an immediate connection between the competency and their learning. When it came time to reflect on these competencies and dispositions, track progress, curate evidence of growth, and communicate with others how these competencies are coming along, students would look at the prompts and reflect on their connections and achievements. These prompts included:

Critical Thinking looks like . . .

- Thinking ahead
- Digging into learning
- Logical thinking
- Learning from mistakes
- Doing research
- Being inquisitive
- Analyzing your thoughts
- Triangulating your research and findings
- Getting uncomfortable in your thinking
- Not accepting things for what they are
- Looking for many opinions and perspectives to create your own
- Doing your due diligence
- Working hard to think
- Flexing your thinking muscle

Collaboration looks like . . .

- Actively listening
- Open-mindedness
- Constructively criticizing
- Teamwork
- Engaging and disengaging
- Positively reinforcing
- Communication
- Clarity
- Self-control
- Strong organizational skills
- Asking questions
- Flexibility
- Patience
- Getting along with others
- Not getting along with others (at times)

Communication looks like . . .

- Sharing ideas
- Asking questions
- Active listening
- Being able to work with and involve others
- Not discarding other's ideas
- Being engaged (mental and physically)
- Being ready to engage with others
- Speaking in turn
- Being respectful
- Openly voicing your thoughts and opinions
- Expressing yourself with detail and clarity
- Speaking to and with others and not at them

- Writing, speaking, showing, creating, and digital literacy—all literacies

Creativity looks like . . .

- Thinking outside of the box
- Alternative learning methods
- Unique presentation styles
- Sharing your ideas with others
- Experimenting with different mediums
- Self-expression
- Taking inspiration from others
- Using your environment, surroundings, and resources to create
- Creativity is found in all shapes and forms
- Surrounding yourself with inspiration
- Divergent thinking
- Coming to a problem from a multitude of angles and perspectives

Empathy looks like . . .

- Being mindful of others' feelings
- Being open to how you feel and sharing your feelings
- Respecting privacy
- Being able to step into the shoes of others, and being able to react accordingly
- Decentring yourself to centre another person
- Showing interest
- Being encouraging
- Showing gratitude that the person opened up
- Acknowledging another's pain or their feelings
- Being supportive

- Enacting change
- Trying to come to a place where you can understand
- Creating space
- Asking how they are feeling
- Being true to yourself

Self-Control looks like . . .

- Being able to limit yourself
- Being able to manage your actions, emotions, and feelings
- Being able to self-regulate
- Being disciplined
- Keeping a level head
- Being able to recognize what you must control and what you can indulge in
- Recognizing why you need to control yourself
- Knowing your limits
- Recognizing what you can't control
- Taking care of yourself
- Having strategies to help in certain situations and circumstances

Curiosity looks like . . .

- Having a strong desire to know or learn about something
- Having an interest in learning
- Being inquisitive
- Caution: "curiosity killed the cat"
- Reading and researching
- Questioning
- Inquisitive thinking
- Investigating, exploring, and discovering

- Talking to people with more knowledge on the subject, seeking an expert
- Inquiring into something
- Getting lost in the learning and losing track of time
- Getting into "the flow"
- Loving learning, loving what you're doing

This process is further explored in Chapter 5, "Set Personalized Goals and Plan the Process."

DEMONSTRATIONS OF LEARNING

I often ask my students, "If you could show me your learning in any way, how would you show me what you know?" My hope is to honour the diverse learners in the room whilst simultaneously leaning into students' strengths when it comes to agency.

Inevitably students tell me the things they have always done in school.

Similar to the list of items on a menu I referenced at the onset of this chapter, I have observed that students don't reflect on this prompt with the depth, individuality, or creativity I would hope the opportunity offers. That's why it's so important that I share with students any artifacts I have curated from other classes and previous years to help paint the picture of what is possible in their learning. I have these artifacts posted on my walls, on display on my shelves, and saved as digital files so I can do a bit of a show-and-share.

By seeing how other students have shown their learning, my students' minds open to the possibilities.

The result of this sharing is that students learn that in our classroom, they will have some voice and choice in how they show their learning and that they can really lean into their strengths and interests. This creates a start point in learning from a strength-based stance rather than a deficit-based position. Kids will choose things that they're good at, interested in exploring more meaningfully, and are more genuinely engaged in. A co-design process allows this to happen.

Some demonstrations of learning will no doubt remain teacher selected, but there is so much room in our curriculum to have students show us what they know in a manner that interests them, engages them, challenges them, and gives them confidence. Allow them to show you!

> In inquiry, students begin to see themselves as a driving force behind the curriculum as they explore and discover learning from a strength-based and relevance-rich stance.

Whenever possible I attempt to categorize and cluster the choices students are making. As I see commonalities and trends emerge, I synthesize ideas and plan from these means; for example, if students would like to demonstrate their learning by creating a series of videos, then I can plan a few mini-lessons, curate some resources, and brainstorm some challenges they may encounter. In doing so, I am supporting them in this agency over their learning.

ASSESSMENT TOOLS

Bringing assessment into the classroom and having it be something we do *with* students rather than *to* students begins with co-designing, and in this specific context, co-designing assessment tools. In my experience, spending time building rubrics with students will create clarity over assessment (students will have a deeper understanding of what they're being assessed on) whilst increasing achievement (the time spent discussing assessment will impact the learning they share). It is time well spent because it lays the foundation for a partnership in assessment that will result in more agency over learning over time.

Consider any mandated rubric you will use with students. Rather than merely bringing that rubric into your classroom and giving it to students to help bring clarity to the assessment, tack this master rubric to the side of your desk and walk students through the following co-design activity instead.

Begin by sharing with students that they will build the assessment tool with you. You may even want to tell them that although you have the tool already, you would like to gauge their understanding of the task and learning goals. The point, of course, is that the assessment tool is something they understand. To ensure that happens, it should be written in their own words. They can then use the assessment to help them find accuracy and clarity.

In pairs or groups of three, ask students to build out their own single-column rubric considering two things. First, ask them to consider what big ideas will be assessed. These will be the categories or rows of the rubric. Second, ask them to consider what language they will include to bring shape to the assessment. These will fill the column and each cell within each row.

As students work on their rubrics, walk through the classroom and observe the activity and discussions. What do you notice? Are student rubrics aligned with what you have on your desk? If not, what are they missing? What specific language do the rubrics students are building need?

Take note of what could help bring accuracy and alignment to the good work that is happening before you. Consider pausing the activity and highlighting some examples of aligned language or student rubrics that could help other groups in their work. Consider having students walk through the room themselves, taking notice of what they see that could shape their own rubric building.

At some point in this activity, I may decide some added support and scaffolding may help the co-design process align the students' work with the master rubric. If this is the case, I use two main scaffolding tools: exemplars and sample vocabularies.

First, I use exemplars that I have kept from previous classes or we have curated as a faculty to help students in this co-design process. I have exemplars for nearly every type of demonstration of understanding you can imagine. I keep ones that are examples of high achievement, ones that need some revision, and ones that received a lot of feedback and support from the teachers. It's important that students see this spectrum during the activity so that they can more clearly and concisely articulate their assessment language and fine-tune their assessment compass.

Typically, I structure several rounds of examining, critiquing, and analyzing the exemplars for roughly five minutes per round. Students are given a sample to pick apart, and I prompt them to add language to the rubrics they are building. At times I may draw their attention to specific details or features of the exemplars if students are missing the mark or require support. At times there may be the need for a few groups to work with the exemplars while some groups do not. I differentiate accordingly and walk through the room providing specific and intentional feedback as needed.

Second, I share a word bank with the class comprising vocabulary words that are on the master rubric. I encourage students to reflect on whether they have used these words in their rubrics and how they could include this language in their work.

This gives me an opportunity to ensure alignment and assessment accuracy whilst giving students the opportunity to have a voice in assessment. This co-design activity creates a partnership between the teacher and the student, one in which we, with time, modeling, and planning, give agency over assessment to our students.

I have written about other co-design activities at length in my first book, *Dive into Inquiry*. It is worth a visit if you would like to add to the breadth of your co-design repertoire. Specifically, I outline how to co-design what effective teaching looks like so our students have a voice in sharing with me what I can do to best support them and meet their needs. I also outline how to co-design your course syllabus. Although there is a lot of "must-do and must-know" in our curriculum, there is also a lot of space for us to connect the curriculum with student curiosities, wonders, and interests.

#INQUIRYMINDSET IN ACTION

For each of the co-design activities outlined in this chapter, plan a series of guiding questions you feel would support the discussion with your students in your specific context. By reflecting on what questions you can ask in advance of the activity, you'll be better able to facilitate the discussion and navigate the sharing of learning. Consider what responses your students will have and how you may draw out more from them by using the guiding questions you are reflecting on. Have these guiding questions at the ready as you plan for this activity in your unit design. You'll be much more likely to feel comfortable and confident in sharing the decision-making process with your students when you have these guiding questions prepared.

THE POWER OF TALK
IN ASSESSMENT

One of the largest and most powerful shifts I have made in my teaching has been toward the power of talk. Facilitating small-group sharing, helping students gain the language of reflection and introspection, nurturing the conditions in which all students feel confident in voice and class discourse, and embracing the intimacy of one-on-one conferencing to discuss thinking, learning, and goalsetting all come to mind as ways I have adopted more talk in my assessment process.

Whoever is doing the talking
is likely doing the learning.

Talk guides my planning, shapes my direct instruction, and informs my teaching. The more powerfully I can facilitate talk, the better I can determine what my students know. All of my teaching stems from the learner first:

- What do students know?
- What prior knowledge do they have?
- What strengths and challenges will be a part of each of their experiences in learning?

I can use the answers to these questions to make informed decisions about next steps. Gathering this evidence can be tricky. I need to know what is in each of my student's heads to teach them effectively. In a class of diverse learners, some confident and others shy, some proficient language speakers and others foreign language speakers, and some from affluent families and others with impoverished home lives, hearing from everyone in the room is a huge undertaking. The power of talk in assessment, when done right, provides the conditions for me to be successful in this endeavour.

In my experience, there are many ways through which we can scaffold talk to support students in sharing their voice and gaining confidence. Each of the following ideas helps ensure that we are hearing from everyone in our classrooms:

START SMALL

I love small-group formations of three. With groups this size, students are more likely to participate and stay engaged. The size provides a level of trust and intimacy that enables students to connect and share. Furthermore, no one voice is likely to be drowned out by another, because the small size encourages balanced involvement from all participants.

Many of our learners are introverted, shy, or less open to public communication and discussion. A small, student-selected group setting that is built on trust and relationship allows students who may feel reluctant to share aloud to the larger group to confidently share their ideas. I position small groups throughout my classroom in a design that allows me to easily and comfortably work with students in a highly personalized manner. I can (and often do) pull up a chair and sit in on student discussions.

At times I may prompt groups with guiding questions to aid their chat and get them thinking about their thinking. Here are a few guiding questions I use:

- What was something you heard that was compelling?
- How can you summarize what your groupmates have said?
- How is what you're hearing different from your thinking? How is what you're hearing the same?
- Is there a way you feel you can help make your group's chat stronger? How?
- If you had to order the group's chat from "mic-drop ideas" to "meh ideas," what would this order be? Why would you order it as such?
- How can you summarize your "mic drops" to another group? Why have you declared it a "mic-drop idea"?
- What resonated with you most from what your groupmates shared?
- How is your thinking different now that you've heard everyone in your group share?
- What are your next steps in your learning? How can you move on from here to deepen your understanding and move forward?
- If you could go and ask another group a question, what would you ask? Why would you ask them this?

I may also provide strategies to help groups overcome a challenge or barrier in learning and to help order or make sense of their thinking. I may suggest one or more of the following strategies:

- Take two minutes to get yourselves prepared for sharing. You could review your notes, reflect on the prompts, or quietly rehearse what you'll contribute.
- Consider actively listening, really focusing on what your peers are contributing. Be present physically as well as mentally.
- Think of one question you can ask to push the conversation forward.
- Document the conversation by writing notes or drawing the big ideas you've heard as they're happening.
- Continually reflect on what you're hearing, and try to put it into your own words.
- Use the reflection stems on the board to help seamlessly slide into the conversation.
- After someone has spoken, honour their contribution by recognizing their thinking and highlighting something they said that resonated with you.
- For ELL students: Consider writing down words you don't understand and then using your translator to help with your next steps.
- If you're having trouble focusing, try using a fidget or some sort of object to help quiet the noise outside of the conversation so you can get the most from what is being shared.
- Physically lean in to the conversation. Sit toward the end of your chair, lean on your elbows, give eye contact, get contemplative, and focus on the words from your peers.

Or I may simply provide praise for their sharing and willingness to discuss their learning so openly with words like these:

- I know sharing aloud is challenging for some. I'm proud of you!
- I've seen how far you've come over the past few months. Good on ya!
- You contributed powerfully to that group discussion. Kudos!
- I loved your responses throughout that sharing. Well done!
- I could tell you were absolutely engaged throughout the chat. Epic!
- Your guiding questions were so helpful to your group. Thanks for that!
- You tend to get the best out of others. That is such an admirable trait!
- I love how caring and welcoming you are of your group-mates. That's rare to see!

And at times no words are needed, especially for those students who prefer the non-public type of praise. I can give a simple smile or nod of recognition to let them know how much I appreciate them.

Sometimes I don't even sit in a group because I can so easily walk through the room, hear their sharing, and immediately know they are on the right track. That they get it. Whatever I do in this situation, it is enabled by the small, self-selected group dynamic.

Another strategy I have adopted during group discussion time is to document feedback and anecdotal evidence as I walk through the room. I keep a notebook handy in which I collect information from what I am witnessing. I try to jot down a few notes on each student throughout each week. I record the date and a summary of the activity and then document anything I see that I can use to provide context during a student conference or on a report card comment. It is always short form and highly personalized.

I also adopt a simple three-point scale to document what I am witnessing. This is especially helpful when it comes to giving feedback on competencies such as communication or collaboration. I also love the three-point scale because it is efficient and timely: I can give immediate feedback that students can take and use right away. As I walk through the room, I simply record what I am observing, and then I can use these observations to give students some feedback.

This small-group structure is critical when it comes to determining what I need to teach next. Powerful and sustained inquiry balances direct instruction with exploration, discovery, student agency, voice, and choice. Inquiry is not one without the other. A significant challenge for the inquiry teacher is to ascertain what should be learned by way of direct instruction and what can be learned by way of exploration and discovery. This balance is one I am constantly mindful of and questioning. Gathering evidence from everyone in the room, not just my brightest or most confident students, in a safe manner and on an ongoing basis, day to day, hour to hour, minute to minute, is a role I happily wear as an inquiry teacher.

Everything in my classroom begins with what my learners already know. This, in turn, allows me to take planned, intentional steps from a position of where each of my students are. Small groups, quick checks, and voice from everyone allows me to make these next steps in an informed manner so that successful learning occurs.

SCAFFOLD TOWARD LARGE

Whenever I facilitate a class discussion, I typically only hear from a handful of students. I'm certain you've had similar experiences. The hands that go up are the same ones over and over again. Despite my encouragement, scaffolding, and eventual prodding, I more often than not leave a class discussion wondering *what was wrong with that lesson? Are most of my students shy? If a group discussion doesn't work, how can I gain an understanding of what they understand?*

I have found that students are reluctant to share for a number of valid reasons. Some students, as noted, are shy and introverted. The thought of speaking up in class causes anxiety and stress. When it comes to better meeting their needs, it is unfair of me to call on them to share their understanding in such a public format.

Some students are reluctant to share in a group discussion because it happens too fast. While they are focusing on processing the question and making sense of what is being asked of them, the class is whirling by in a myriad of sharing and group discourse. By the time they've gathered their thoughts and have formed an opinion that they feel is worthy of sharing, the time to share has passed.

Some students have become complacent during group discussions. They have figured out that if they remain patient and appear engaged, someone else in the class will raise their hand instead of them. These students are playing the waiting game. They are waiting for the teacher to "pick on" someone else. They are waiting out their peers, hoping one of them will cave in first and raise their hand. These students view group discussion as a game, and they play it well.

To curb the outcome of students not participating, I always lead in to group discussions through small group chats as outlined above. The obvious benefit of trust and open discourse is one of the reasons I do so. The other rests in the opportunity to leverage rehearsal time.

REHEARSAL TIME

Rehearsal time occurs when I prompt small groups to have one member volunteer to share something from their small group to our larger class discussion. I always provide three to five minutes of rehearsal time before this larger group share. This time allows volunteers to gather their thoughts, connect with their peers, and formulate a clear, concise, and on-topic response. If I feel it is necessary or helpful, I draft a few rehearsal stems on our whiteboard for students to use in their sharing, such as the following:

- My partners _____ and _____ and I discussed . . .
- My partners _____ and _____ thought the most important thing that was shared was . . . My partner _____ shared that . . .
- I appreciated when my partner _____ said . . .
- My thinking was different from my partner ___ and ___'s because . . .
- Some of our thinking changed when our partner _____ said . . .

We then hear from all of the volunteers, with one representative from each group speaking.

At the start of the school year, the benefit of rehearsal time isn't necessarily tangible. The students who volunteer are usually the same students who would have raised their hands to participate in a class discussion anyhow. For the most part, they're confident, extroverted, and willing to openly share their opinion. The benefit of rehearsal time begins to be seen partway through the year, after several months of continuously scaffolding and supporting students to gather their thoughts, connect with their peers, and formulate a clear, concise, and on-topic response.

Eventually, different volunteers participate, and the benefit of the time we have invested in hearing from *everyone* becomes evident. Students know they can trust a group discussion, that I will never call on them blindly, that I will always give them time to get prepared, that their voice matters, and that they *all* have something important to contribute to the collective.

Rehearsal time creates the trust students crave so that they feel confident enough to be vulnerable and share their thoughts. It also provides the time, skills, and understandings required to communicate to a larger group.

Equitable entry points into learning allow all students to thrive and discover belonging in the classroom.

FLIP CLASS DISCUSSION WITH FLIPGRID

Another method I employ to scaffold toward larger class discussions is leveraging the power of Flipgrid. I am a huge Flipgrid fan. Of all the tech advancements in the classroom over the course of my career, Flipgrid, by far, has had the greatest impact on my assessment practice. This platform has a soft spot in my heart for a few reasons. One, it's free. And when I say "free" I mean free: no charges for extra features, full access, or greater capacity. The entire platform costs users, both teachers and students, nothing. This sort of equity in the educational technology market is rare and welcomed.

Two, it truly amplifies learning and empowers student voice, something near and dear to my teaching philosophy. Flipgrid is a video-response platform in which you and your students post topics, record responses to prompts, reply, and collaborate. The platform fosters confidence and ownership over sharing one's voice. Students begin to take ownership within the platform as they interact with their peers, providing feedback, advice, and insight into one another's wonderings and reflections.

Three, Flipgrid is easy to use and intuitive. Teachers can easily and safely send prompts to a classroom that is protected by a code or password. If so desired, teachers can safely invite other students or parents into this space to see the recordings. Students appreciate the opportunity to record and re-record until they are ready to publish their thinking. This is something that sharing aloud in a traditional classroom setting doesn't allow. Flipgrid ensures that students can share something they are proud of.

Let me share with you how Flipgrid has specifically impacted my assessment practice. Recently my students wrote and performed original slam poems that reflected their identity. I've done this assignment before, but it changed dramatically with the advent of Flipgrid. I gave students the option of performing their slam poems in front of the class as a spoken language presentation or as a recording to our Flipgrid space. Almost unanimously students choose to record using Flipgrid.

In the days leading up to our due date for this assignment, a student named Hudson published his slam poem early. He came to class on a Friday, quite proud of himself, announcing to me (and anyone within earshot) that his poem had been posted and that he eagerly looked forward to my feedback. Seeing as the due date wasn't until the Monday after the weekend, everyone in the class now had the opportunity to watch Hudson's poem. What followed was truly eye opening to us all.

By the time we returned to class on Monday, Hudson's video had been viewed by his classmates close to 300 times! The number of views, however, only tells one layer to this story. Students who watched Hudson's video also gave him powerful feedback in the form of a reply to his slam poem. Many students left Hudson praise for his performance or constructive advice on how they felt he could improve his piece. This was unsolicited from Hudson as well as unassigned by me. Classmates felt compelled to interact with one another within the platform because of the collaboration Flipgrid fostered as well as the reflection before publishing that it demanded.

When Hudson returned to class on Monday, he was full of thanks for the feedback he received from his peers. He was also excited to re-record, given the clarity he gained through their praise and suggestions. Again, this was entirely unassigned. By the time I assessed Hudson's slam poem, he had re-done it several times, with dozens of comments from his peers and hundreds of views from our class. This type of concentrated and meaningful feedback would just not be possible if Hudson had performed his slam poem in real time for us all. He would have had one chance to do well, with no opportunity to reflect and revise. The performance anxiety under these circumstances can be overwhelming to many of students. Flipgrid allowed me to gain a much clearer assessment of Hudson's abilities, and his product was something he was proud of. Undeniably this is better for everyone involved.

Here are a few other ways I enjoy using Flipgrid in my assessments:

- **I give each of my students their own private grid where they can post thoughts, reflections, or responses to my prompts.** I find this incredibly rewarding, because students will be more honest and open about their learning when they know there aren't others listening. They aren't concerned with judgement or saying something for group validation. Their recordings are genuine. As such, I gain a clear understanding of whatever it is they are sharing. The student can invite others into their grid via a password or invitation; however, most won't. They value, as I do, the ongoing one-on-one conversation we have about their learning. They enjoy reflecting on their posts over time. They view their grid as a digital portfolio, a vehicle collecting the process of their learning throughout the year.

- **I ask students to record a conversation together.** In groups of two, I ask them to introduce themselves and then participate in a conversation stemming from a provided prompt, where they can demonstrate communication and collaboration. This is a neat activity because it transcends the content of our curriculum and focuses on competencies (collaboration, communication, problem-solving, creative thinking, and so forth). Students plan more than what they'll say. They plan how they'll say it, to ensure that they demonstrate collaboration and communication. I often witness powerful collaboration and communication at work before the recording is even completed. This aids my assessment in that I am aiming to gather a performance of every student in a timely manner that alleviates the performance anxiety of completing the task in front of their peers.

SPIDER WEB DISCUSSIONS

I absolutely adore the work of Alexis Wiggins. Her Spider Web Discussion framework for fostering student discussions has created some of the most enthusiastic class discourse I've witnessed. Similar to Socratic seminar, Spider Web Discussion places students in the centre of the learning process as the teacher becomes more of a silent observer and recorder of what they see students saying and doing during the activity. Spider Web Discussions have also allowed me to collect evidence on the depth to which my students communicate with one another.

It can be challenging to assess a competency for depth: What is the spectrum of communication? What does one student communicating better than another student look like? Is there a particular frequency at which stronger communication is attained? Wiggins' work through Spider Web Discussions sheds light on these questions in a fun, achievable, and applicable framework.

Spider Web Discussions scaffold into class collaboration and communication through several clear steps: objective setting, designing criteria, selecting a rich and engaging provocation, and facilitating a roundtable style discussion. I have made slight modifications to Wiggins' process in that my students and I set objectives and design criteria together, as we do throughout all assessments in the inquiry classroom.

What I love about the Spider Web Discussion framework is that it truly puts students in the driver's seat of class discourse. The class is temporarily designed for a Spider Web Discussion, with desks in the shape of a circle or oval. This allows for clear eye contact and easy communication. When I facilitate a Spider Web Discussion, I quietly position myself outside the circle, far enough away that I am physically removed from the discussion yet close enough that I have a clear line of vision that allows me to observe everyone participating. I remind students that, in the time provided, they are to try their best to achieve everything we have set out as objectives and within our co-designed criteria. Then I observe the discussion from my position outside the circle, allowing students to take on authentic leadership roles within a collaborative and trusting dynamic.

I busily take notes and track the discussion using a unique web graph that is a reflection of the seating arrangement including student names, a few abbreviations to help aid me in jotting down observations, and a space for notes and summarizing. Each time we do a Spider Web Discussion, I use a new web graph to document the activity and compare against previous web graphs. Over time the web graphs change, reflecting a balancing of discourse and an equity in roles. Eventually everyone becomes a leader, a listener, and a more complete collaborator and communicator than earlier in the year.

I have witnessed numerous benefits from Spider Web Discussions in my classroom that, similar to the design of a spider web, have ties to other, sometimes unforeseen, benefits. First, students demonstrate growth across several competencies. Whether collaboration and communication, as noted, or others such as problem solving and critical thinking, personal and social awareness, or creative and divergent thinking, students have an opportunity to become proficient across all of these areas. Learners are constantly exercising the collaboration muscle, and they stretch and grow as communicators. Confidence increases as they begin to take on more ownership in the classroom, an ownership that leads to a strengthening of community, building of trust, and nurturing a culture of collaborative inquiry that, in my experience, is otherwise difficult to achieve.

Spider Web Discussions also provide me with better assessment data. Using the web graph and abbreviations, I can track behaviours and competencies, look for contributions, examine for patterns, and take notes on whether participation advances discussion or stifles it. I can give timely feedback immediately after a Spider Web Discussion, or I can simply display my web graph via our class projector and have students self-assess or collaboratively assess what the data tell them. Again, Spider Web Discussions foster agency because the framework puts students in the driver's seat of their learning.

Let's take a closer look at Spider Web Discussions through the lens of the author herself, Alexis Wiggins, in this contribution to *Inquiry Mindset*:

Spider Web Discussion is something that developed in my classroom while teaching at a Harkness school just outside New York City. The Harkness Method is a method of student-led, problem-based discussion that began in the early 20th century at a prep school in New England called Phillips Exeter Academy, known simply as Exeter. Decades ago, Exeter was looking for a better way for their young men to learn than raising hands and giving the answer to the teacher. Harkness was born out of this search for a better way to learn; it asks students to be seated in an oval so that everyone can see everyone else, and the learning—whether in science, literature, or any subect or school context—happens through student-led discussion.

My experience at a Harkness school was fascinating, working with students who were encouraged to lead their own inquiry. But I began to see ways to inspire even deeper learning through a unique assessment practice and feedback process, developing not only students' ability to inquire but also to lead and empathize. As I say in my book, we ask students to collaborate together all the time, but how often do we actually assess the quality and effectiveness of their collaboration?

Prior to developing Spider Web Discussion, I did what most teachers do with regard to participation: I counted it as a small percentage of students' grades, which ensured that talkative students earned high participation grades and shier, quieter students struggled to earn top participation marks. But developing Spider Web Discussion as a method that asks all students to participate (more or less) equally forced me to confront the fact that I had been rewarding bad behavior for years. I had been rewarding students for volume, not quality. Students who spoke often had higher participation grades, and students who spoke less had lower ones, but until I developed SWD, I didn't have a mechanism to help them understand how to improve the quality of their participation. And the truth is, a well-timed question by a quieter student might lead us to much deeper inquiry than ten opinions shared by a student who loves to hear herself talk. If I want balanced, rich, collaborative inquiry, then I need to have specific feedback mechanisms for showing students when their contributions are helpful in moving the conversation forward and when they hold us back.

Now, students in my classroom learn to lead the discussion while I observe off to the side. At the end of the discussion, I use my notes—maps of the discussion and questions or comments I want to highlight or follow-up on—to lead them through the feedback process. Sometimes the feedback is more focused on content, ideas, or questions about the topic that warrant more exploration. Sometimes, though, the feedback is more focused on process—what happened when Allison asked that question and everyone suddenly wanted to contribute? How can we do more of that? How did we miss Zev's reference to the quote that provided good context? How can we make sure we don't miss his contributions next time? How can we do better next time? Using a formative group grade and a clear, straightforward rubric that students can self-assess against easily helps us all understand that we were on the same team, trying to collaboratively move the ball toward the goal.

When I first employed this method in my classroom for discussions, I expected to have more balance and better-quality discussions, and I did. But I didn't anticipate a couple of the other benefits: First of all, we really needed everyone to bring their A-game every day. If students showed up without their work done, it was quickly apparent in the discussion; they either couldn't contribute or made superficial or unhelpful comments that didn't deepen the inquiry. While students might generally be okay with disappointing the teacher by not doing homework, I found that they are much less likely to disappoint their peers. In Spider Web Discussion, we are all counting on you. Without you, we can't have our best discussion. As one French teacher who tried the method and fell in love with it told me: "All the slackers do their homework now!"

Secondly, and more importantly, I found that the method deeply and permanently shifted my classroom culture. Because there was more intentional listening and building on each other's ideas, there was an outgrowth of empathy. Students were no longer talking over each other or fighting to get their word in edgewise, which is the typical Socratic seminar structure with individual participation grades. With a group assessment, students now understand that their leadership is about inviting others into the fold, drawing out the best of each other, not only themselves. Students ask thoughtful questions; they apologize when they interrupt, and they ask quieter students their opinions. They notice who has spoken less and quiet down when he is about to speak. They listen more, understanding that participation and leadership is sometimes more about listening than speaking. Couldn't the world use more leaders like that?

Spider Web Discussion is just one path to inquiry, not the only one. There are many great discussion tools out there for teachers, but I have been sharing this one in my writing and presenting for over a decade because it is the single most powerful tool I've found in my teaching toolbox. When teachers let go of their role of deliverer of content or arbiter of discussions and think of themselves as coach of a team, there is a power-ful shift in the classroom. Students want to treat others, and be treated themselves, as intellectual equals. They want to be ethical and effective communicators. They want to be collab-orative leaders and inquirers. Spider Web Discussion is a way to help students become all of these things, and all it requires is sitting in an oval and following a simple rubric. As I always say to teachers in schools and at conferences where I present on the method, just try it once and see if it doesn't excite and surprise you. It might just be the best class you never taught.

THINKING ROUTINES

Another educator who has had a great impact on my practice is Ron Ritchhart. Ron's work at Harvard Project Zero and his ongoing commitment to the development of intellectual character, creative teaching, and making students' thinking visible is deeply tied to my work in inquiry. Ron is a part of a broad school of thinking, a collec-tive that is interested in advancing student agency in schools around the world. This body of work, of which Ron is a part, has inspired my inquiry practice with both students and with teachers. See the suggested reading list for more amazing educators who are a part of this school of thinking.

One aspect of Ron's offering I wish to surface here is thinking routines. Thinking routines "operate as tools to prompt and pro-mote thinking, as structures that reveal and scaffold thinking, and through their use over time become patterns of behaviour." These thinking routines are a set of making thinking visible practices that collectively provide the educator with a direction for empowering students to understand themselves as learners and thinkers whilst the educator gathers information through questioning, listening, and documenting. As students reflect and grow and thrive, the teacher simultaneously reflects and grows and thrives to better meet the needs of the students in the room. Ron's work is powerful stuff! Here are a few thinking routines that come to mind:

Give One Get One (GOGO) gets students up and moving about the classroom, sharing ideas and actively listening to classmates with a critical lens to deepen understanding around a predetermined topic or prompt. In my experience, this routine is lively, engaging, and informative. As students walk and connect and share, they compare their own thinking with others, soundboarding ideas and pinging thoughts back and forth with one another, adding compelling ideas to their own list and contributing their ideas to that of their classmates.

The routine concludes with an opportunity for students to unpack the experience within small groups or the broader class. They are prompted to explain, justify, or connect their ideas with what they heard from their classmates.

The result is not just that students have a richer list of ideas at the conclusion of the routine. Students are refining their thinking as they critically analyze the ideas of others whilst critiquing their own ideas. Furthermore, students flex several competencies throughout the routine with collaboration, communication, and critical thinking. Teachers gain invaluable information on where their students are and where they need to go next. They have ample opportunity to pause the routine, coach and model a move, behaviour, or thought, or hold up a student conversation to guide the experience for others.

Question Sorts help inquiry practitioners and students organize questions to determine which are worthy of investigation and will have the rigor, shelf life, and interest to lead to deeper and sustained inquiry.

The routine requires a large set of questions on a concept the class will explore and discuss. Dan Rothstein and Luz Santana's Question Formulation Technique (QFT) is a questioning protocol to help generate questions whilst nurturing the competency of questioning with students. It is one way in which students I support in inquiry generate the questions we grapple with using this thinking routine. Consider using the QFT to help you in this regard.

Once a set of questions about a concept has been generated, students are prompted to sort their questions using an X- and Y-axis on the whiteboard by writing their questions on sticky notes and posting them in the shared graph. The X axis is generativity: How likely is the question to engage, challenge, provoke, and lead to deeper understanding? The Y axis is genuineness: how much does the group care about investigating the question? Include two additional lines from the middle of both axes to create four quadrants within the graph. This will help sort the questions further in terms of "high" and "low" for each category.

As questions are posted and discussion ensues, students are prompted to step back and take notice of what has been shared. The upper right quadrant represents the questions students have decided are the most generative to explore and that they most genuinely care about. I enjoy dissecting the type of questions in each quadrant and calling on students to share what they notice, what they observe, and what they think. As with the GOGO routine, the competencies that are flexed during the Question Sorts routine are abundant. Again, critical thinking, collaboration, and communication come to mind, as do empathy and curiosity. Thinking routines, in my experience, are not a series of isolated tasks or activities. They are a part of a series of behaviours and beliefs that simultaneously make thinking visible, strengthen student agency, and honour competency development.

I Used to Think, Now I Think is an absolute favourite routine of mine when it comes to infusing more student voice in our assessment work together. This routine calls on students to reflect on their learning throughout a unit of inquiry or span of time and consider how and why their thinking has changed. It gets students thinking about the process of learning and not merely the product of learning. They get critical about the evidence, resources, and artifacts that shaped their thinking, impacted their learning, and made an impression on them.

Like all of Ron Ritchhart's thinking routines, they enable students to flex a variety of competencies as they engage in the routine. Here, students are examining, analyzing, synthesizing, connecting, and finally, explaining, all rich examples of the critical thinking and communication competencies at work.

In my experience, it's important that students are called on to document their thinking early and throughout the unit of inquiry so that they gather a rich and robust collection of learning evidence they can dip into during this thinking routine. I call on students to keep as much learning evidence as possible from all aspects of their learning. They should keep artifacts they are proud of, that highlight their strengths and successes in learning. But they should not limit themselves to just the "great evidence." They should include the messiness of their learning too. The artifacts also should reflect the challenges they faced, the trouble they encountered in learning, the difficulties they grappled with, and their reflections on these rich learning experiences. By keeping hold of all forms of evidence, students will have a powerful array of evidence to speak to using this thinking routine.

As I mentioned, this thinking routine is a favourite of mine. I'll refer to it more in Chapter 12, "The Power of Student Voice in Reporting."

#INQUIRYMINDSET IN ACTION

In reflecting on the variety of ideas in this chapter on how you can bring more student talk into the classroom, consider which of these already has a home in your practice, which is something you are aware of but can bring some more intentionality to doing more often in your classroom, and which of these ideas is new to you and would be something you would like to add into your inquiry repertoire to elevate your teaching and impact the student experience.

SET PERSONALIZED GOALS AND PLAN THE PROCESS

When I visit schools around the world to help them implement inquiry with their students, I often refer to the sketchnote below. The 10 Characteristics of the Inquiry Classroom sketchnote is the result of a fun collaboration with educator and sketchnoter extraordinaire Sylvia Duckworth. It represents years of working with teachers in inquiry with their students. Throughout my career, I have tried to capture what I see in these inquiry-driven classrooms, asking, *What does inquiry-based learning look like? What do inquiry teachers do? What do students learn in an inquiry classroom?* This sketchnote captures these observations and brings them to life through the power of imagery. Have a look!

10 Characteristics of the Inquiry Classroom

@Trev_Mackenzie   @sylviaduckworth

1. Nurture student passions & talents

2. Empower student voice & honour student choice

3. Increase motivation and engagement

4. Foster curiosity and a love for learning

5. Teach grit, perseverence, growth mindset & self-regulation

6. Make research meaningful & develop strong research skills

7. Deepen understanding to go beyond memorizing facts and content

8. Fortify the importance of asking good questions

9. Enable students to take ownership over their own learning and to reach their goals

10. Solve the problems of tomorrow in the classrooms of today

Genius Hour ♥ 20% Time Passion Projects

In watching teachers in inquiry with students, I saw these characteristics surface repeatedly. These characteristics do not necessarily pop up in a single lesson nor at the same time in an inquiry classroom. But over a span of time, perhaps in the course of several weeks, all of these characteristics eventually show up in the inquiry classroom.

When working with teachers, I use this image as a reflection tool. It serves as a sort of personalized diagnostic exercise to help teachers determine where they are in their inquiry teaching and where they want to elevate their inquiry skill set. Teachers reflect on the image and share which characteristics they feel they do well, the characteristics that are a strong part of their inquiry repertoire. They include examples of how these self-described inquiry strengths surface in their teaching. I then ask teachers to consider which single characteristic they would like to focus on improving as a professional learning goal for the future weeks and months of their inquiry teaching. I always leave each attendee with a takeaway resource to help them make this goal a reality.

Time and again, one of the most commonly identified goals is Number 5: *Teach grit, perseverance, growth mindset, and self-regulation.* Teachers from all over the world ask, "What is grit? How do you teach students about the value of a growth mindset? How can we nurture perseverance in our classrooms?"

With these incredibly important questions in mind, we design lessons and intentionally plan experiences and activities that help their students understand the value of grit, perseverance, growth mindset, and self-regulation. The outcome is that their students become agents over their assessment and, in turn, agents over their learning. Undeniably, the most powerful and effective way teachers can nurture a growth mindset and sharpen self-regulation in students is through their assessment practice. It is through a partnership in assessment, reflection, and evaluation that students learn to try again and again, until they master their goals. This display of per-severance—of not giving up or giving in—is *grit*.

> The most powerful and helpful way we can nurture a growth mindset and sharpen student self-regulation is through our assessment practice.

Let's take a look at how grit develops in my classroom. At the beginning of the school year, I always ask students what goals they have for their learning. I find this conversation and the data I collect to be immensely helpful in several ways. First, I value gaining a better understanding of who my students are and what they hope to gain from our time together. I want to know how their curiosities, passions, and interests can potentially shape both *what* we learn and *how* we learn it. Second, when it comes to successfully nurturing a culture of inquiry, getting to know my learners during our first days and weeks together is of the utmost importance. Identifying their goals helps set the stage for a culture of inquiry that is guided, in large part, by the students in the room. And third, this conversation helps me get to know them as learners, the strengths and challenges they bring to the classroom, and how I can better meet their needs throughout the school year. They feel better supported, and I feel better equipped to support them.

To set the stage for a rich and meaningful conversation about their goals for learning, I sometimes rely on the work of psychologist and author Angela Duckworth. I am a huge fan of her powerful research and writing, as she sheds light on the role of perseverance in learning, a characteristic she has coined as *grit*. Duckworth demystifies the reasons some people stick with tasks through difficulty and hardship more than others. Her work is especially important when it comes to the field of education. As a teacher, I have often wondered, *Can we teach grit? Can we nurture the conditions that promote perseverance in learning?* And as a learner I wonder, *How gritty am I?* and *How can I become more gritty?*

To explore these questions as a class, we watch a clip from Angela Duckworth's compelling TED Talk, "Grit: The Power of Passion and Perseverance." I encourage you to watch the video in full, but I've found that minutes 3:00 to 5:30 have been the most interesting to my students.

Scan the QR to watch the video.

The video provides some direction for us to begin reflecting on our own learning strengths and challenges. In small groups, we discuss what from the clip resonated with each student. I ask students to share examples to their group of when they've demonstrated grit, whether they feel they are gritty in certain areas of life more than others, and whether they feel they've become grittier over time. Their discussions always reveal fascinating information that continues to inform my teaching.

Angela Duckworth Grit Scale

I then introduce students to Duckworth's grit scale, a short survey that calls on participants to reflect on their own learning and to what extent they possess grit. Students independently complete the survey and tally up their scores, which provide a general idea of where each student is on the grit scale. You can find the grit scale at angeladuckworth.com/grit-scale. I encourage you to use the scale for yourself and tally up your own score.

As we consider where we each fall on the grit scale, I refer my students to our co-designed competencies posted in our classroom. These competencies provide reflection points for students throughout the year and give students some of the language they will use when setting individualized goals. Learners enjoy reflecting on these competencies because they transcend the content and subject matter of our curriculum. The competencies are the overarching learning goals of our year. Students understand that it is in sharpening these competencies that the skills and understandings of becoming lifelong learners can be obtained.

I ask students to identify the competencies they feel they do well or possess to a strong degree. I also ask that they provide some evidence of how these strengths are demonstrated in their learning. I encourage students to provide evidence from any area of life and not just in the context of school or a particular subject area. In this regard, I do not want students to have a misconception that creativity, for example, only happens in art class. We often demonstrate creativity in many areas in life, and part of my role is to help facilitate experiences in which creativity occurs more often within the school setting.

I then ask students to identify a single competency that they will focus on elevating and sharpening throughout the upcoming term. This competency will represent their term goal. I request that they develop a strategy that will help them to meet this goal. As students are reflecting and sharing in small groups, I wander through the room and provide examples of strategies where needed; for example, if a student has identified that their term goal is to become a better collaborator, but they are struggling to identify a strategy to help them work toward improving in this area, I might ask them to consider focusing on active listening when collaborating, or to provide supportive feedback and encouragement to their peers when collaborating.

My support is important, but it is equally important that I do not merely tell my students what their goals are or tell them what their strategies should be. At its essence, this is a co-designing activity in which I support my students and guide them through the process. This is a critical step in students becoming more comfortable in taking on more agency over assessment.

I keep the process from being confusing or overwhelming by not giving them too many choices and by providing necessary support. The list of competencies combined with the offering of a range of strategies help students feel confident and informed. By the end of the lesson, students have identified a few strengths as well as a single goal and accompanying strategy for the term.

As outlined in Chapter 3, Co-Design and Co-Construct, each of our competencies is displayed in our classroom as a large poster illustration that students created. These posters are displayed in the classroom so all students can see them and reflect on them at any point in the inquiry. We add to these posters during this goal-setting activity. I prompt students to create their own bitmoji avatar, a personalized emoji that we will print off and post on the competency that they've set as their goal. I ask students to create a bitmoji that demonstrates them focused on a task, working toward a goal, or putting their specific competency in action. I share a Google Slides deck with the class and give all students editing access to add their bitmoji too.

Here are avatars that I've created for myself as examples and several from students who recently completed this process:

These bitmojis represent so much more than merely a cute and fun activity. Each bitmoji characterizes each student's personalized goal and commitment to working toward their competency development. The highly visible bitmojis provide me a constant visual reminder as to what each student is working on; therefore, I can pause at any given moment in learning to reference a particular student's goal and mention something I am noticing in their growth. The highly visible bitmojis also provide students with a simple reminder each time they glance up at their competency poster to reflect on their learning and how *what* we are learning about is tied to their personalized learning goal and *how* they learn.

As you will see in the next chapter as I outline reflection guiding questions, these bitmojis give us all the opportunity to capitalize on co-designing learning together whilst encouraging student agency over assessment.

We then begin to connect the two parts of the lesson, Duckworth's grit scale and the students' competency goals, to set the foundation for our ongoing commitment to becoming lifelong learners and resilient citizens. Duckworth's research, her TED Talk video, and the grit scale all provide powerful context that allow the competencies to come to life for students. I record their grit scale scores, their identified strengths, and their single competency goal and supporting strategy so that I can refer to them throughout the year as I prompt students to reflect during the learning process. I may prompt them by asking, "Over the course of the last week of learning, what circumstance illustrates how you grew toward achieving your competency goal?" Or if we have been working with partners and in small groups, I might say, "Throughout the collaborative experiences you've encountered over the past weeks, describe opportunities in which you feel like you have grown as a learner."

> Consider asking your students to bring a photo of themselves from home instead of going through this bitmoji exercise. A photo from home can be meaningful and special for all involved, including parents when they come in for student-led conferences, parent/teacher night, or our open house/inquiry gala event.

Here are some more specific competency reflection prompts that I use throughout the year:

- What is a form of communication that you are proud of? What is it about this form of communication that you are proud of?
- How do you share ideas and communicate with others?
- What is a strategy you use when you disagree with someone? Where did you learn this strategy?
- How do you generate new ideas? What sort of environment inspires this type of thinking for you?
- Describe a time that you designed something. What did it feel like?
- When you are curious, how do you find answers to your questions?
- How do you ensure that the information you discover online is valid and authentic?
- Describe a time you overcame a challenge. What did you learn from this situation?
- How would you describe yourself? What shapes your identity?
- How do you demonstrate empathy, compassion, and kindness? Describe a time where you helped someone else. What did you learn from this experience?
- What does creativity mean to you? Describe a time when you demonstrated creativity.
- How is it possible to solve a problem in different ways? Have you ever demonstrated this?
- How have you demonstrated responsibility?
- Describe a time that you solved a problem. What strategies did you use to help you overcome this challenge?

- Describe a time when you felt you were a part of something larger than yourself.
- How do you value the past? How can we use the past to shape our future?
- How do your actions impact others, either positively or negatively?

My students' reflections serve as powerful personal narratives that I often include in report card comments, as portfolio evidence, or as summative reflections on behalf of the students. I continually revisit prompts like these throughout the year because they shift our focus to the process of learning rather than a perceived or prescribed destination. The reflection reinforces that growth and success are personalized and different for each learner, which gradually moves us away from a comparison assessment culture to one of individual fulfillment and meaning. Finally, it takes us to an assessment conversation that transcends the content by having us talk about who we are as people.

I conclude the goal-setting activity by asking students to identify the grade they hope to acquire by the end of the term and school year. This is an important conversation to have. Although there is incredible strength in framing learning around self-regulation and competencies, the frustrating reality for teachers is that we are still required to provide a mark at the end of each reporting period. Whether it be a letter grade or a percentage point or an SAT score, assessment data are still widely used to help organizations categorize students and quantify learning. In my experience, as students reflect on self-regulation and competencies throughout the year, they simultaneously home in on their academic goal mark. The two are inherently connected, and as such, my intention is to support growth in both realms by facilitating the conversation and reflection as outlined here.

The specific mark or grade each student has identified provides me the opportunity to personalize feedback for each learner I work with. It helps us both be accountable and focused when it comes to persevering and being gritty. It lets me know where they'd like to be by the end of the year, and with that information in mind, I can help them identify clear and helpful steps in making their individual goals a reality.

The feedback I provide each student is personalized to help them meet their individualized goal. I no longer need to hold students accountable to unrealistic and, at times, unhealthy expectations; for example, if a student's goal mark is 88 percent and they have achieved this mark on a particular assignment, I first give them congratulatory comments about having attained their goal. In their eyes, 88 percent is just as good as 100 percent, and as such, their work and efforts should be celebrated.

Of course, I also provide students with clear and meaningful feedback on how they can continue to improve their work; however, this feedback comes after my congratulatory comments. Students begin to read feedback from a position of being honoured and celebrated rather than from a deficit mindset or from a place of feeling that they're not good enough. A positive mindset, after all, is incredibly empowering when it comes to understanding oneself as a learner. Furthermore, it helps us break down the comparison culture of assessment all too often prevalent in our schools.

#INQUIRYMINDSET IN ACTION

How can you bring self-regulation to the conversation with your students? What picture books, videos, stories, texts, or other resources can you include in this goal-setting process in lieu of Angela Duckworth's resources? As you continue to co-design learning with students, is there a particular competency goal that you can set for yourself and make visible alongside your students so they can see you work toward your own goal? How might you share the challenges that you've encountered as you pursue your goal, identify strategies that you've applied to your learning, and pause to coach and model your growth over time for your students?

ASKING THE RIGHT QUESTIONS

Questions provide a path to and for inquiry. They spark curiosity and sharpen your students' critical thinking skills. The most effective in the inquiry classroom require *pondering* rather than internet searching, which is why we refer to them as *unGoogleable*. I've written at length about the role and power of questions in *Dive into Inquiry* and *Inquiry Mindset: Elementary Edition*. For this book, however, I want to focus on using questions to scaffold toward increased student agency over assessment. In this chapter, we'll explore several of the ways you can elevate your questioning focus within your inquiry practice.

USE QUESTIONS TO FRAME YOUR INQUIRY UNIT DESIGN

Begin planning your unGoogleable question by considering the overarching concept, big idea, or deep understanding you are aiming for with your inquiry. Write this concept as a word or phrase, and then spend some time creating the question that will frame your inquiry. Your planning should be focused on deepening an understanding of this question; for example, in exploring the concept of identity in the language arts setting, an inquiry-framing question could be *who are you and what shapes your identity?* In unpacking the concept of change in the social studies or history setting, an inquiry-framing question could be *how can we learn from our past to shape our future?* In learning about the concept of predicting in the science setting, an inquiry-framing question could be *how can you use the scientific method to challenge your ideas about reality?* Finally, the concept of relations and patterns in maths can be explored in an inquiry-framing question such as *how can you use logic and patterns to create a game to be played by and enjoyed by others?*

I enjoy using the Question Formulation Technique to create questions, and it is best to have students involved in the process. Remember, one goal in an inquiry classroom is to continually co-design learning together. Allowing student participation in the planning helps bring the curriculum to life. As they add their questions to the unit, they explore and discover authenticity in the inquiry.

Student-generated questions bring the curriculum to life by having them explore and discover authenticity in the inquiry.

Co-designing your learning units with your students' questions avoids repetition and "cookie cutter" inquiry across a grade level or faculty planning team. More importantly, it ensures that your students are engaged in and excited about the learning going on in your classroom.

Imagine this scenario: In a planning session, a team of teachers selects a concept they will all build an inquiry around. They construct the unGoogleable question together. They design the exploratory questions students will research to deepen their understanding of the unGoogleable question. They research a provocation to spark curiosity and wonder in the inquiry. They even plan some of the resources that students will grapple with and explore in the inquiry.

Although this scenario is a great example of collaborative staff planning, it is void of the most important stakeholders in our schools and the most critical voice in the co-design process: our students.

Now imagine this scenario: In a planning session, a team of teachers selects a concept they will all build an inquiry around. By selecting a unified concept, they can support one another in ideas, resources, and even cross-class collaborative inquiry. Teachers take this concept back to their students and brainstorm questions together, slowly with planning and discussion and collaboration. Perhaps using the Question Formulation Technique, the class identifies an unGoogleable question of their own as well as exploratory questions they will research to deepen their understanding of the unGoogleable question. Teachers then come back together and share what surfaced in their classrooms, what they noticed and observed in the experience of co-designing with students, what their unGoogleable question is, and where the inquiry, for now, is directed. Teachers can then collaborate with one another on provocations, resources, guiding questions, and competency development across the inquiries that are being planned.

One of these scenarios is co-designed with students, and one is not. The scenario that is co-designed with students is more likely to yield higher engagement, increased authenticity, and connections to the student experience—all of which combine to make a greater impact on student learning and achievement.

When settling on the unGoogleable question, teachers and students should keep these four factors in mind:

1. The unGoogleable question should be compelling, engaging, and interesting to the students.
2. The unGoogleable question should be authentic, contextual, and easily tied to the place, community, or world around your students.
3. The unGoogleable question should be one in which your students can successfully explore, and for which you have resources or research pathways or supportive learning friends that would aid you all in deepening your understanding of the unGoogleable question.
4. The unGoogleable question should belong in your curriculum. It should be a question that aligns with the learning objectives, standards, and goals.

The unGoogleable question cannot be something that doesn't meet each of these factors.

MAKE QUESTIONS VISIBLE IN THE CLASSROOM

Once you've settled on your unGoogleable question, consider making it a focal point in your classroom. I post each unit of inquiry's unGoogleable question at the front of the room above our whiteboard in a nice large font. This visual provides a clear, constant anchoring of our learning throughout the inquiry. It allows me to pause learning, point to the unGoogleable question, and make connections between whatever we are reading, exploring, examining, or discussing to the overarching question and concept of the inquiry. This coaching and modeling also empower students to take agency over their learning by encouraging them to make connections to the unGoogleable question on their own. I love watching the mental lightbulbs switch on when they make a discovery of their own. Making the unGoogleable question visible is a critical step in supporting students be successful in inquiry.

Additionally, I have a designated bulletin board or wall space in the classroom for each unit of inquiry. The board consists of the unGoogleable question we explored surrounded by evidence and artifacts from the learning within that particular unit. It is a learning evidence board that all students contribute to throughout the inquiry. It allows students to learn from one another's contributions to the board and acts as an anchoring space for their thinking, both collaboratively and individually.

For each unit of inquiry, we create an individual inquiry board. The rich learning display can consist of student-selected proof of learning as well as evidence that I assigned and collected throughout the unit of inquiry.

To elevate these individual inquiry boards, I tie a line (e.g., string, fishing line, or yarn) across the classroom overhead, ideally a few feet above a standing adult, depending on the height of the room. Students are encouraged to make connections across the inquiry boards, create artifacts that represent the connections they have made, and clothespin these artifacts to the line. Over time a web of connections and rich, student-centred artifacts begins to emerge and decorate the space. It's a lovely sight! Have a look at these two examples from my dear inquiry friend (and coauthor of *Inquiry*

Mindset: Nurturing the Dreams, Wonders & Curiosities of Our Youngest Learners), Rebecca Bathurst-Hunt:

When parents are invited for student-led conferences, parent/ teacher night, or any open house or gala at our school, students are invited to speak about their contributions to the inquiry boards and connections. I use these contributions, discussions, and the rich sharing that occurs as part of my assessment practice. The authenticity, student engagement, and centring of the student voice creates an equitable entry point for all students to be successful.

Authenticity, student engagement, and the centring of the student voice create an equitable entry point for all students to be successful.

Another great example of how to make questions visible comes from inquiry friends Hollie Parker and Stephanie Sewell, year five teachers at St. James Lutheran College in Queensland, Australia. I have had the fortunate opportunity to support this amazing school in its inquiry journey. The school takes a collaborative and inclusive approach to learning, with open classrooms occupied by two classes of students, two teachers, and a learning assistant. The contemporary spaces and flexibility to be creative and collaborative with the curriculum allow teachers to embrace inquiry while catering to individual needs and learning differences.

Hollie and Stephanie use the walls in their classroom to visibly map out prior knowledge, interests, and curiosities and, eventually, misconceptions. Hollie and Stephanie had this to say about their inquiry classroom:

> *Misconceptions are all around us, ever present in our lives. Providing our learners with the opportunity to identify and unpack misconceptions further develops their ability to solve problems—academically, socially, and emotionally.*
>
> *Sometimes, posing a simple question or series of questions structured around a concept we will be exploring can*

ignite student interest and enable prior knowledge to massively influence the direction of an inquiry. We begin our new units of inquiry by posing two questions, and our learners are provided with a visual space to map out their reflections and track their progress.

The first question is, what do you know? This invitation to learning presents a starting point to guide our learners to gain an understanding of the concept we will be inquiring about. From here, many learners are excited to discover that their prior knowledge is strong. They are all given sticky notes and provided with time to reflect on what they know.

Our second question is, what do you want to know? Learners are provided with a stimulus to invigorate their curiosity. They are then given additional sticky notes and asked to reflect on what they want to know about the given concept. We share these and post them on our visual learning map for all to see and reflect on.

This is when the magic happens!

Our researching, exploring, and digging begins at this juncture. Throughout this process, learners are encouraged to reflect on their prior knowledge, and slowly, some learners will begin questioning themselves and what they shared to the wall under the What do you know? *space. With scaffolding and encouragement, they begin digging a bit deeper and ultimately realize that some of their prior knowledge may have been misconceived.*

Obviously, this isn't always the case; however, when these connections are made, the pride and awe of our learners is palpable. Our learners can then move their misconception from the What do you know? *space (or rather, what they thought they knew) to a new* Misconceptions *space on the visual learning map. The goal here is not only to gain knowl-edge, but also to cultivate and create lifelong learners who are prepared to take risks and show their learning process whilst being influenced by their curiosity and challenged by their misconceptions.*

Over time we have realized that our learners have had little exposure to the concept of misconceptions. Part of the process that we have strengthened has been to intentionally scaffold and teach what a misconception is. Our learners are now at a point in their inquiry journey where they can iden-tify misconceptions in a variety of contexts, from literacy to maths, science and HASS [Humanities and Social Sciences], right through to critically questioning their social and emo-tional learning.

GUIDING QUESTIONS ARE THE SECRET SAUCE

Learning to plan for and use guiding questions to help create more student agency in the classroom has been a pivotal piece of my inquiry practice. As I plan for inquiry, I include a dedicated space in my unit and lesson planning for the guiding questions I may use when learning occurs. I consider a number of things when planning these guiding questions, including who my learners are, what their strengths and stretches are, and what they are interested in learning.

Learner Identity

- Who are my learners?
- What is their story and experience?
- What cultural elements do they bring to the classroom to make the learning richer for all?

- What guiding questions can I ask to surface the unique qualities, characteristics, and identities of everyone in the room?
- How can I create opportunities for all students to contribute their perspectives and insights to the inquiry and discovery process?
- How can my guiding questions create equity in the learning?

Learner Strengths and Stretches

- What strengths does each student bring to the inquiry?
- How would they like to show me what they know?
- How do they prefer to take in information?
- What competencies and dispositions do they have in their inquiry toolkit?
- What would stretch them in this particular inquiry?
- What challenges do I anticipate each student could encounter in the inquiry?
- What guiding questions could I ask to help each student reflect on their individual strengths and stretches to help them be more successful in the inquiry?

Learner Interests, Wonderings, and Curiosity

- What interests each of my students?
- What are their passions and hobbies?
- What would they be curious about in this inquiry?
- What do I know about them that could help us discover authenticity and engagement in the inquiry?
- What would they like to know or do with the concept our inquiry centres around?

- In knowing my students, how could I spark curiosity and interest in the concept through the lens of exploring and discovering the inquiry?

I use guiding questions in both my planning of the inquiry when I am alone and when I am planning the inquiry with my students. Consider every guiding question I referenced in the above sections. Each one can be posed directly to your class to shed light on how you can co-design your unit of inquiry with increased student voice. Guiding questions bring planning, intentionality, coaching, modeling, and a learning partnership to the inquiry. Guiding questions simultaneously engage students in the planning of the inquiry whilst informing you of how to best meet the needs of the students in your classroom.

Finally, I use guiding questions to help students reflect on their learning and understand themselves better. I share with students that I value the process of reflection and that I'll continually give them the time, space, and structure to think about themselves as learners, to set goals, and to work toward meeting these goals.

As an English teacher, it is natural for me to ask students to reflect on their learning in written form, as a journal or free write task; however, this format should not be solely housed in the English stream of our schools. All classrooms should provide students with the time, space, and structure to reflect on their learning. The act of thinking back on the process of learning and documenting growth over time is valuable in all subject areas, classrooms, and faculties. Students will make cross-curricular connections when we provide them the opportunity to reflect on their learning in all spaces in our schools.

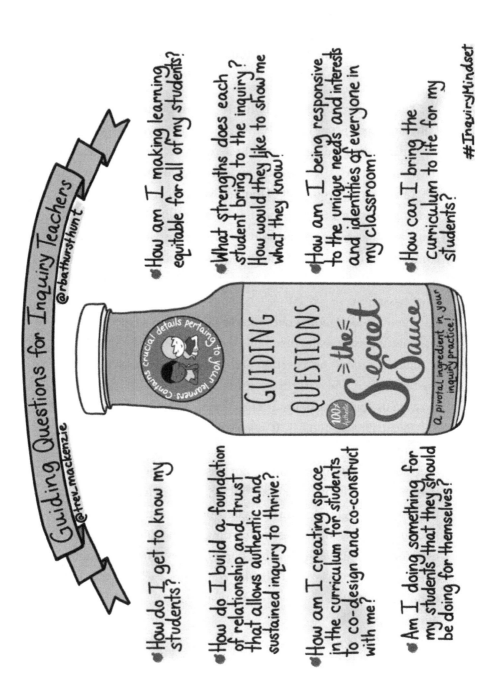

All classrooms should provide students with the time, space, and structure to reflect on their learning. The act of thinking back on the process of learning and documenting growth over time transcends all subject areas and classrooms and faculties.

When students think about their thinking and are given the language of metacognition, they inevitably become stronger learners. They understand what works for them, what challenges them, and what they need when they set goals for themselves. It's in the process of reflecting on some of the specific prompts I provide that students embark on this process of getting to know themselves better.

Here are some guiding questions that I propose to help students reflect on their learning:

- What was a challenge you encountered in your learning?
- What is a strategy (or series of strategies) you used to help you overcome this challenge?
- Was there someone you leaned on or learned from throughout your learning? Who was it? What did you learn? How did they help you?
- What competencies did you flex throughout the learning? What evidence can you speak to that demonstrates these competencies?
- What competencies did you grow in? How did this occur? Is there still room for growth with regard to this competency?

- Use the thinking routine "I used to think . . . Now I think" (as referenced in Chapter 4, "The Power of Talk in Assessment"). Provide some examples to shape your thinking as well as language from our unit of inquiry.
- Was there an area within our inquiry unit where you feel you could have done better? What was it? How could you have done better?
- In reflecting on your research, what sources proved fruitful in your learning? What sources were not as helpful? What research skills did you use in your inquiry?

The writing and sharing from these guiding questions help get students primed for reflecting when it comes to the final step of the 10 Steps to Nurture Student Ownership Over Assessment: student voice in reporting. To scaffold for this level of agency over assessment, reflection and guiding questions are a critical component that we coach and model and structure.

#INQUIRYMINDSET IN ACTION

In reflecting on the role of questions in inquiry to impact student engagement and achievement, what additional guiding questions would help your students in the classroom? What questions could you have at the ready to support students in their growth and development? What questions do you anticipate would help shape the direction of your inquiry? What questions could you ask to help your students dig into reflection? What questions do you currently have in your inquiry repertoire?

FLIP THE FEEDBACK

"Formative assessment is not a task. Formative assessment is an ongoing, embedded practice that allows teachers to constantly make adjustments to their teaching based on what they're observing. Feedback is a mindset."
—Ron Ritchhart, *Inquiry Live*

"Feedback is not advice, praise, or evaluation. Feedback is information. Feedback is information about how we are doing in our efforts to reach a goal."
—Grant Wiggins

"If students know a classroom is a safe place to make mistakes, they are more likely to use feedback for learning."
—Dylan William

"When we give grades as part of our feedback, students routinely read only as far as the grade."
—Peter Johnston

"Students need to know their learning target—the specific skill they're supposed to learn—or else 'feedback' is just someone telling them what to do."
—Susan Brookhart

"Effective feedback occurs during the learning, when there is still time to act on it."
—Jan Chappuis

wholeheartedly agree with and use each of the preceding tenets on feedback to guide my practice. And there's one more that I want to share . . .

One of the most successful assessment routines I have used in my career occurred while grappling with feedback. It came as a result of the frustration I felt every time I returned an assignment to a class. After spending hours reading student work, assessing student learning, drafting clear, helpful, and personalized feedback—all with the goal of pushing learning forward—I noticed that students were only interested in their mark. Time and time again, I would hand back assignments requesting that students read the feedback I provided and plan a course of revision to demonstrate growth and impact achievement. Each time, students ignored my pleas and the potential for growth I saw for them. They ignored the feedback and quickly flipped right to their mark. They would then turn to a friend or peer and, in whispers, compare marks. It was frustrating and heartbreaking.

There was no soaking in or understanding of the feedback.

There was no revision or growth mindset being demonstrated.

There was no point in providing the feedback if it wasn't going to be used.

Have you had a similar experience?

Then, one day I read Dylan William's *Embedded Formative Assessment,* and his words pushed me to do something different because they rang so true: "As soon as students get a grade, the learning stops."

That's when I flipped the mark to focus on the feedback.

My goal was to try something different—to see whether I could get students to use the feedback and, perhaps, gain a better understanding of their learning in the process. I decided to continue to provide the rich and helpful feedback I had in the past but chose to not provide a mark on their assignment. Rather, I would record their mark in my gradebook and have students participate in a self-assessment reflection activity.

I challenged students to closely read the feedback I gave them. I shared that this feedback reflected my assessment of what they had done well and what they could do to improve, if so desired. I asked them to compare this feedback with the co-designed rubric we had established before the assignment. I suggested that if my feedback was clear, on topic, and balanced (not too much praise yet not too much of the constructive feedback), they would be able to use our co-designed rubric and determine the mark I had recorded in my gradebook. If they self-assessed drastically lower or higher than the mark I recorded, we would both know that my feedback was not clear, on topic, or balanced. In these cases, I would need to review the feedback I had given and provide clarity or further support to aid their growth and improvement.

> When it comes to feedback, ask yourself: is my feedback clear, on topic, and balanced?

The impact on their learning was immediate. Students dove into my feedback with gusto. They examined my assessment. They reviewed the co-designed rubric. They discussed and compared their feedback with their group. At times they read one another's assessments to lend support and provide clarity. It was awesome to watch—and completely unexpected. In my entire career, I had never seen students examine feedback so intently. These students were *into* it.

I knew we were onto something special.

As my students reviewed the feedback and self-assessed using the co-designed rubric, I walked throughout the classroom and listened to the conversations amongst the groups. I could hear them talk about their learning, and I observed a certain positivity in the room, a tone that let me know students were not only enjoying the new assessment process, but that it was likely having a positive impact on them. My hope was that this activity would slowly break down the comparison culture of assessment so common in classrooms, replacing it with an experience that would strengthen the skill of reflection. Even more, I wanted to help students understand themselves better whilst reducing the stress, anxiety, and fear of failure that traditional assessment routines had caused them.

I wanted students to feel better about themselves as they received feedback about their learning, not worse. And with this flipped feedback, I saw the difference immediately.

Students were smiling as they enjoyed the assessment activity. (Yes, they *enjoyed* assessment. Who would have thought *that* was possible?) Students inquisitively dug into the feedback and compared it with our co-designed rubric. They collaborated as they shared feedback with friends and worked together examining the co-designed rubric.

I then asked students to record the mark they felt was warranted by the feedback. I asked them to share this mark with me one-on-one so as to provide some space from wandering eyes and comparing peers. Students and I looked at both marks, the one they had chosen after reflecting on the feedback I had provided and the one I had recorded in my gradebook. For most of my students, the two scores were remarkably similar. Most of my students could use the feedback to clearly determine their own grade using our co-designed criteria. Talk about student agency!

For the few students whose marks were dissimilar to mine, it became clear on reviewing the feedback I had provided that I had been either too hard on them or not celebratory enough in my remarks. I revised my feedback and clarified my error with them. Students enjoyed the human element to the process and how assessment became something they were involved in rather than something that was done to them. They enjoyed having a conversation about their learning.

A few students required deeper explanation and clarification, because my mark was different from theirs, and my feedback was clear, on topic, and balanced. When this misalignment surfaced, I viewed it as an opportunity to sharpen my student's assessment compass for accuracy, clarity, and rigor. In my experience, there are always a few students who, for one reason or another, require some added time to grapple with this process, with me supporting them along the way. This is not a failure of the process. This is an opportunity to better meet the needs of these students.

Having done this exercise many times now, I anticipate all of these conversations and scaffold for them. I make sure that my learners know that I am aiming to sharpen their assessment compass. I want them to see this activity—and assessment as a whole—as a partnership and a process in which they will be actively engaged. After all, teachers are the assessment experts in the room. We have been assessing our entire careers. We must coach and model assessment skills for accuracy, clarity, and rigor so that students can slowly become better assessors and eventually learn to accurately self-assess in any context.

Teachers must coach and model assessment skills for accuracy, clarity, and rigor, with the goal of empowering students to accurately self-assess in any context.

This activity had several immediate impacts. First, it ensured that my feedback was clear and helpful and was being reviewed and understood by the students. I really had to consider my comments to ensure that my notes were in student-friendly language. As a result, my feedback became much more focused and personalized. The activity provided me with a new layer of intentionality and removed any chance that the time we invested in assessment was wasted. The goal for my feedback was clear: it had to help students understand where they were, where they needed to go next, and how they could go about getting there.

Second, this activity created a powerful balance over assessment between the teacher and the student. Learners became more engaged in reflecting on their learning and more motivated to push forward as they used my feedback to improve their marks. In this activity, assessment was a two-way street. Assessment was a partnership. No longer was the assessment expert merely me, the teacher. Students understood assessment to a degree that allowed them to take more ownership over their learning.

Third, this activity broke down the comparison culture of assessment all too evident in our schools. In my experience, students do not compare marks throughout this activity. One obvious reason for this is that, at first, they simply don't have a mark to compare. Even after students leave our one-on-one conference, I do not hear the whispers of comparison or see the slumped shoulders of defeat that typically occur in other assessment processes. Students leave the conference with an enthusiasm for the reflection accomplished and the work ahead. They are keen to take their feedback and apply it to their learning. The activity promotes the tenets of growth mindset I aim to nurture by way of my assessment practice.

Of course, I follow up this activity by providing a bit of time for students to make changes to their work. Knowing that powerful learning has already occurred in the form of meaningful reflection and accurate self-assessment, I am flexible in when students demonstrate their growth through revision. Timely revision is important, so I encourage students to demonstrate revision within an hour after the activity. If students require more time, however, I give it. For me, the important growth is in the action of reflection and accurate self-assessment. It is not whether one student gets it done sooner or earlier or faster than another.

Whatever your school context, grade level, or subject area, holding off on giving your students a mark or grade and narrowing their focus on understanding and acting on feedback holds incredible promise. Nothing is worth grading unless students are given helpful and clear feedback, teachers have ensured that students understand the feedback, and students have the time and support to act on the feedback. Please consider this as a foundational process in your assessment practice.

#INQUIRYMINDSET IN ACTION

Plan for this feedback activity within an upcoming unit of inquiry you are currently planning. Plan for the time it takes. Plan for the transparency of scaffolding so students understand that this assessment experience will be unlike other assessment experiences they have had in the past. Plan the prompts you will use to guide your students through the activity. Plan how you will spend time conferring with each student once they have completed their self-assessment using the co-designed rubric. Take the time to bring the intentionality to the process that it warrants so that your students can benefit from this new agency over assessment.

RELATIONSHIPS
PAVE THE WAY

Pretty early in my career I learned of the power of knowing my students. Knowing their interests, their curiosities, and their passions made me a better teacher. Knowing their strengths in learning as well as the barriers and challenges they faced allowed me to better meet their diverse needs. The more time I spent getting to know my kids, the better students they seemed to be. It was magic.

Let that sink in.

The investments educators make in building strong relationships have lasting impacts on our students. They begin to see themselves in the curriculum. They begin to discover authenticity and relevance in their learning. Teachers cultivate a learning environment where students feel safe to take risks and embrace vulnerability for the rich returns of growth and development.

If we are talking about student-centred learning, it's imperative that we are also talking about how we can more actively, intentionally, and consistently decentre ourselves in the classroom to lift up our students.

Accurate, purposeful, and successful self-assessment and peer-assessment are dependent on relationships being built and nurtured, both by teachers with students and with students amongst one another in the classroom.

DATA WE COLLECT

attendance

assessments

report cards

behavioural reports

DATA WE SHOULD COLLECT

their stories

their passions

their interests

their goals

#INQUIRYMINDSET   #DIVEINTOINQUIRY   @TREV_MACKENZIE

With the importance of relationships in mind, I tweeted this image a few years ago. Within a single day, the graphic was retweeted and liked more than 2,000 times. That surprised me. But what really blew my mind was the discourse attached to the tweet. The conversation that occurred, the ideas being shared, and the passion and dedication to teaching that were displayed left me in awe.

What was it about the power of relationships that struck a chord with teachers from around the world?

It's important to note that my belief around the disparity the image suggests isn't an attempt to provoke an either/or debate. Nor did I intend for the graphic to suggest that one is seemingly better or more powerful than the other. The tweet was not an attempt to ignite a conversation about one type of data *over* the other. In truth, the graphic reflects a large part of my philosophy around inquiry and evidencing and how the two types of data should be used to shape our role as educators.

I've always been a teacher driven by action research and data. I reflect on my teaching practice and use my reflections (i.e., data) to inform and guide what I do next, what I revise to move my teaching moving forward, and what I further question to continue to impact my students. The term *data driven* does not hold a negative connotation for me. I have made sure that the data I collect are ultimately shaped by and include the voice and identity of each and every one of my students.

At the heart of the graphic is this question: How do we ensure our students' stories, passions, interests, and goals are woven into our evidencing practice, guide our instruction, and shape our pedagogy?

Lofty ideals and big ideas, I know, but we are in the business of changing lives. Our students have the right to have their voices be a part of their education.

This is why I believe the graphic resonates so deeply with us all. For too long, the first column of data has been overemphasised in education. It's easy to reduce our students to data points and quantitative analysis. It is much more challenging to get to know them, their interests, their curiosities, their strengths, and their challenges.

That reality led me to explore ways that teacher can more meaningfully connect with students. My hope is to shed light on the role of relationships in learning and how we can create a classroom culture rooted in trust and kindness, with the aim of cultivating equity and psychological safety for all.

I have spent much time questioning how the data in the left column would be impacted or altered if we used the data from the right column to guide our practice and shape how we build relationships with our learners. And what I have learned is that when student's stories, passions, interests, and goals are woven into our class culture, our evidencing approach, and our pedagogy, the data in the first column are clearer, more accurate, and truer to the student than ever before.

As I travel the world supporting teachers in implementing an inquiry approach to teaching and learning, I visit many types of schools across a wide array of cultures, languages, and curricula. No matter where I visit or what the school culture is like, we invariably discuss the role of relationship in the classroom. We discuss how strong relationships are created and then nurtured. We explore how we can get to know our kids better and how we can let them know that we *truly see them*. We discuss this image and the two types of data we know are powerfully important in the classroom. It is this work that I would like to share with you.

THREE QUESTIONS TO IDENTIFY A CULTURE OF INQUIRY

1. How do we get to know our students?
2. How do we build a foundation of relationship and trust that allows authentic and sustained inquiry to thrive?

3. How do we build a culture of learning that allows students to feel psychologically safe—a culture in which risk-taking, exploring our vulnerabilities, and finding failure are the norm, and judgement, accusation, and scrutiny are absent?

As I explore these three questions with teachers and students around the globe, the discussions invariably shed light on how we build relationships with our students and with each other. It is in these discussions that each school I support discovers their own culture of inquiry. I'd like to share with you a few of the most meaningful contributions I have encountered. My hope is that you will share these insights to your colleagues and students to help shape the culture of inquiry at your school.

KNOW ME BEFORE YOU TEACH ME

I recently worked with Coomera Rivers State School in Queensland, Australia, supporting them in their inquiry journey. The school has a lot of amazing things going on. They pride themselves on their collective commitment in moving forward with a vision to constantly evolve to reflect the needs of their learners, their community, and the world. They dedicate time in their week for powerful instructional and collegial coaching, time in which teachers collaborate and learn together. They are an Apple Distinguished school and have an impressive bring-your-own-device (BYOD) program that allows for flexibility for learning as well as the potential for differentiation and personalization for students. Students have their own iPads, each installed with a range of suggested educational apps.

The most powerful thing I learned from my time at Coomera Rivers State School, however, is something they call Know Me before

You Teach Me. I asked teacher and learning coordinator Karen Caswell to describe it for us here:

What Does It Mean to Know Me before You Teach Me?

Picture this: It was week one of school and the office photocopier was running hot. Sheet after sheet coming out of the printer reflected some form of diagnostic testing—spelling, number facts, writing, reading comprehension.

Now imagine what that looked like in the classrooms. Students sitting quietly, working independently. Few quality interactions with the teacher or their new classmates. Now imagine how they answered these questions when they arrived home: *How was your day at school? What is your new teacher like? Do you like the other students in your class?*

Our teachers were victims of a crowded curriculum in which every day of learning was important. We didn't disagree. Every day of learning is important, but if there are not positive relationships between the learner, the teacher, and the family, learning cannot be maximized.

We asked our students what they needed during the first week of school, and their responses were a wakeup call. They wanted time to tell their teacher that they were struggling, whether it be with life or with learning. They wanted their teacher to know that they had friendship issues. They wanted their teacher to know that their parents had separated over the break. It was not all doom and gloom. They wanted their teacher and peers to know that they were a good person, a good friend. They wanted to show their teacher what they were good at. They wanted to share their goals for learning. They wanted the opportunity to start fresh with a new year, a new teacher, and a blank slate.

To enable this, we developed Know Me before You Teach Me (KMBYTM). We rearranged the curriculum to enable the first week of school to be completely dedicated to non-curricula experiences that revolved around building relationships between students, teachers, and families. This was a whole-school initiative, and every class participated. We designed fun and engaging opportunities for students to shine.

For example, Know Me as a Writer was a whole-school writing activity using a real-life prompt of Humpty Dumpty. Know Me as a Reader involved a book-tasting, in which students browsed through a range of texts to identify a book of choice. They then developed the class library with their teacher. Know Me as a Person saw students and teachers complete a series of challenge-based activities that promoted opportunities for students to demonstrate team-building skills along with traits that reflect character and citizenship. In this way, we were able to focus on the whole child to nurture all of their qualities, not solely the academic aspect.

What Have Been the Benefits of Know Me before You Teach Me?

Having a whole-school approach ensured that every learner was going home raving about their day at school and so were teachers. It created a sense of belonging and ownership for learners, and we found that they transitioned into learning more easily. Most importantly, our teachers and learners knew each other, and this really became evident when learning became tough and behavioural issues arose. Our students were more willing to push through challenges and were more willing to work with their teacher when solutions needed to be found. Those families who engaged in KMBYTM activities demonstrated open forms of communication. They responded to emails more quickly, they answered the phone when we called, and they attended school events and activities, because they had a trusting relationship with the teacher and the class.

How Would You Like to See This Further Developed at Your School?

In 2021, we are going to build on the success of our first year of Know Me before You Teach Me by incorporating more opportunities to get to know our learners better, such as Know Me as a Creator, and maintain our focus on relationship building throughout the year. Our first unit of inquiry across the school will focus on Identity and Belonging.

Exploring an unGoogleable question through inquiry-based learning, we aim to help students identify their strengths, develop strategies to overcome challenges, understand how personal qualities and positive relationships contribute to success, and appreciate that respect, empathy, and diversity strengthen our identity and belonging, as well as the identity and belonging of others. Our vision is to engage our students in deep learning to foster twenty-first-century citizens who have the character necessary to collaborate, communicate, and think critically and creatively to have a positive impact on their school, community, and the world.

GREET STUDENTS

Students crave a fresh start. They crave the opportunity to begin anew and prove themselves to their teachers. Each and every day, we have the chance to greet them into learning with kindness, understanding, equity, and acceptance. We have the power to be flexible, to be personable, and to be supportive. Time and time again, I have witnessed teachers lead with compassion. And in those moments, I am taken aback by how heartfelt and caring their actions are. We have a chance to give our students a fresh start with our first interaction of the day. What does this look like? How can we use the opportunity before us?

Greet Kids at the Doors to the School

Take a morning a week (or more if you can) and be present at the main door to your school. Greet students. Hold the door open for them, say hello, and make eye contact with them. A point of first contact into the school that is nurturing, assuring, and welcoming sets a positive stage for the day for our learners. When students feel accepted and cared for, the positive ramifications for their learning stretch far. Not only are they more primed for learning for the day, but they recognize that an adult in their school sees them and cares for them. And it's this understanding of acceptance that allows us to cash in on our investment of being present at our front doors.

I recall an incident at my school where this rang especially true. I was walking to the washroom during my prep block when I came across a student who was storming out of another classroom. It was clear that he was pretty upset as he kicked walls and punched the air around him, swearing under his breath and aggressively pulling at his hair. As I got closer, I realized I knew this student. His name was David, and we had a strong bond built from our time together in our English class. I felt fortunate that I came across him when I did. I helped him calm down and listened as the told me about what he was feeling. In listening to David, I was able to convince him to consider talking about what had gotten him so agitated and visiting with one of our school counselors.

As we walked to the counseling office, I did my best to prepare David for what was to come. I told David how friendly and supportive our counselors were. I suggested that sharing a bit of what led him to having such big feelings could be helpful in solving the problem. I described how I sometimes have feelings of being over-whelmed too, and I described some of the strategies I use when these feelings surface. Essentially, I was attempting to lay the groundwork for David to have a successful chat with our counselor. What I hadn't anticipated was that everything I was doing wasn't necessary. As soon as I introduced David to the counselor, his energy changed. Not only did he recognize my colleague, but it was clear he thought highly of him and that there was something that David admired in him even before they had a chance to get to know one another. *What exactly was it? How is this possible?* I wondered.

Each morning at our school, this counselor holds the front door open for kids. He greets them, welcoming them to learning. He cracks jokes. He dishes out high fives and smiles and small acts of kindness. Many of the students who experience his routine don't directly work with him, and most haven't even met him.

One of the students he greeted each day was David. Through this daily act of kindness, our counselor planted the seeds of relationship that eventually grew into something special.

In this case, it was the counselor's steadfast dedication to kind-ness that appealed to David. He saw the counselor as someone he could trust and talk to. If it weren't for the counselor's presence at the front door each morning, David would not have entered into their conversation with such a strong relationship and trust.

A sad truth is that for many of our students the most anxious part of their school day is when they first face walking into our build-ings. Being there for them right away with kindness and acceptance gives them the positivity and confidence required to be primed for learning, whilst providing us with a rich opportunity to better meet their needs.

Greet Kids at Special School Events

I've seen some of the most inspiring scenes in schools when teachers come together to collectively greet students to a school event or on a special day. Whether it's the first day of school or the last, when we celebrate their presence and welcome them with a boisterous round of applause, a cacophony of cheers, or a gauntlet of high fives, a culture of relationship begins to take shape.

Scan the QR to watch the scene.

At McMinnville High School in Oregon, staff line the main corridor of the school to welcome their grade nine students on the first day of school. The result of all this fanfare is that these students gain a sense of belonging. They know they are a part of something special, something greater than themselves. They feel pride in their school, and they know that their teachers care for them. After this sort of welcome, when these students walk into a classroom, they are primed to take on a more meaningful role in their learning because the culture of their school is inclusive of all and founded on kindness and celebration. Thank you to McMinnville Principal Dr. Amy Fast for sharing this video and exemplifying the importance of collaboratively celebrating students and creating a genuine sense of belonging and community.

Greet Kids at Our Classroom Door

Transitions are challenging for our students. Many schools provide a mere five minutes between classes. That's five minutes to transition and to take care of your needs: washroom visit, food break, locker stop, social interaction on the go, and self-regulating and checking in with your own well-being.

It's also five minutes to transition from one teacher's expectations and pedagogical stance to another's. This is of particular importance in the inquiry classroom because students take on a much more active role in their learning, one in which student agency and genuine decision-making are at the forefront of how the class operates.

School systems, timetables, and bell schedules put incredibly challenging, unrealistic demands on our students. Spend a day walking in a student's footsteps: Attend their classes, take their breaks, hang out in the spaces that they typically hang out in. Throughout the experience, take reflection notes as you go. Document your observations. Reflect on your emotions, your focus, and your energy. I anticipate we would all feel rather overwhelmed with what we experience.

I have committed to being at the door of our classroom at every break to welcome students into learning and bid them farewell as they leave. This is harder than it sounds. With the dozens of emails we receive each day, last-minute lesson prep for each class, and the unforeseen demands we constantly experience as teachers, it is difficult to make this work each day. More often than not, however, I make it happen, and my students appreciate this simple act of kindness.

What I value most about greeting my students is that I get an informal check-in with each one of them. I read their body language. I try to assess their feelings. I can gauge their readiness for learning. Before our class has even begun, I am able to make some informed decisions about what I should do next. Simultaneously, greeting students at our classroom door creates a culture of learning that will lead to trust, collaboration, and communication. When students know you care, amazing things happen.

Have a look at this in action with this clip from Edutopia titled *Making Connections with Greetings at the Door*. The video shares a variety of helpful tips and strategies to make the most of our very first interactions with students each day so that we can nurture the conditions to have them feel connected and ready for learning. Whether it is emotional and physical safety, cultural safety and empowerment, or using this first interaction as an opportunity to take notice of our student's readiness for learning, starting the day with an intentional greeting has powerful and lasting benefits.

Scan the QR to watch the video.

Start Slowly

The transition into learning doesn't stop at the door. It continues in the way we spend our time together on any given day. Rarely do I jump right into a lesson without giving students time to settle in, connect with their peers, and get warmed up for learning. Getting students prepped for learning can take many forms. At times it could be a provocation, a rich and engaging entry point into the curriculum to ignite their interest, spark engagement, and capture their curiosity. Provocations can be videos, striking images, interesting artifacts, compelling statements, guest speakers, investigation stations, and even field trips. The list is endless!

Whenever I share a provocation, I ask my students three questions in sequence: What do you notice? What do you wonder? What do you know? This thinking routine allows students to enter learning from an investigative stance, one that immediately activates engagement and questioning. These three questions also provide an opportunity for students to access prior knowledge. Rather than entering a lesson in a passive manner, one in which students consume a lesson from a complacent stance, provocations put students in the driver's seat of their learning, allowing them to engage with the direction of learning and our curriculum in a highly personalized manner. I've written about provocations in *Inquiry Mindset Elementary Edition*. Consider expanding your reading on the topic there.

Starting slowly can also come in the form of a reflection prompt. Reflection prompts typically touch on the previous day's wonderings, the overarching big idea, an unGoogleable question we are exploring, or the concept we are deepening our understanding of. Reflection prompts can also provide an opportunity to tune into how students are feeling. This further aids in smoothing the transition between classes (and teachers) whilst giving students time and space to assess their readiness for learning and self-regulate from there.

A reflection prompt can also be a quick turn-and-face activity during which I ask students to share their reflection to a partner. I can wander through the room and check on conversations, gather some great information on how students are doing, where they are in their learning, and how I can best support them in moving forward. Reflection prompts can even be recorded digitally or via pen and paper to be added to a student's portfolio of learning. Gathering evidence of learning and making thinking visible gives students a chance to revisit these important steps in the process of learning when it comes time for a summative conversation about their thinking.

GO OUTSIDE TO COME BACK INSIDE

The stuff that happens outside of class matters, and more often than not, it's the stuff that helps us discover relevance and powerful start points to inquiry. Whether it is an extracurricular activity, a family event or trip, something exciting that happened over the weekend, or simply acknowledging that their lives outside of class are important, students want to know that we care about their interests, their curiosities, and their passions.

As of late, a big shift I have made in my teaching has been trying my best to attend school events. Music recitals, sports games, drama performances, robotics competitions, club fundraisers, or whatever the focus may be, I try my best to show up and support students. I often take my elementary-aged children with me in the hope that they will be inspired by all of the opportunities that await them when they attend the high school where I teach.

Very few of my students even notice when I'm in attendance at a basketball game or a music recital, but that's not the point. The good stuff occurs in the follow-up the next day, when I see a student in class who had a fantastic game or a great performance, and I congratulate them on their awesomeness. They appreciate that I recognize their commitment to something outside of schoolwork and assignments—something about which they are passionate. They are genuinely thankful for the support, and they enjoy knowing that I see their talents. Later on in the year when it comes time to explore an interest, curiosity, or passion as part our free inquiry unit, these interactions prove to be quite beneficial to me, because I can suggest inquiry pathways or concepts based on what I've learned about the students outside of our class time together.

Going outside to come back inside has another meaning for me. It represents going outside my comfort zone when it comes to letting kids into my world outside of the classroom. It means becoming more confident taking the time to discuss things that are beyond the curriculum, the things that allow the curriculum to come to life. It means opening up my story so my students can feel more confident as they write theirs. I used to be hesitant to share my own story and my interests, curiosities, and passions with students. I thought my "work life" and my "school life" should be separate.

Kids don't want to hear about my hobbies and passions. They would think these are boring. Why would students care about what I enjoy doing in my spare time?

It's unprofessional talking about things outside of our curriculum.

It's taken me a long time to become comfortable sharing more of myself with my students. I've come to realize that informal interactions throughout our time together can be the glue that strengthens our relationship and helps build our collective culture of inquiry. I keep a few things in mind when it comes to sharing with students:

Be honest. Students can smell inauthenticity from a mile away. Always leading with the truth matters. Demonstrating vulnerability, fear of failure, and my own uncertainties in the classroom all help students see me as a learner—like them. This creates trust and a willingness to explore their own vulnerabilities, fears of failure, and uncertainties in the classroom. It is often through these interactions that I am able to model my grit, perseverance, and growth mindset. Students can learn a lot from our experience. When we allow ourselves to be honest and vulnerable as we share our stories, they grow confidence in sharing their own.

Be professional. I reserve the right to say no thanks or to refuse to divulge more of myself than I am comfortable. Letting students into my life and what I love doing outside of class is important, but not if it is inappropriate. As such I always maintain a professional line of discourse with my students.

Be passionate. Students need to see passion in action. They need to be around teachers who are passionate about teaching and have big questions and curiosities of their own. These big questions may well be tied to something I am exploring as a teacher to expand my inquiry repertoire. Letting kids see how passionate I am to try something new together gets them excited and willing to try it out, too.

The passions you share with students can also come from outside the classroom. As I talk about my passion, I articulate the trials and tribulations that come with pursuing excellence with something you love. I explain that passions don't happen overnight. Passion arises because we stick with something for a long time, through the trials and tribulations of learning, until there comes a day when we find ourselves *needing to do it*. Passions start as small questions, curiosities, or interests and, over time, with the support of others and our commitment to sticking with it, we begin to love what we are setting our mind to.

Be human. If my lesson falls apart, I admit defeat. If I'm feeling stressed, I put words to it. If I'm not feeling up to the task, I articulate my uncertainties. And if I need a break, I invite my class to take one with me. Being a passionate teacher is something I strive to demonstrate each day, but being a perfect teacher is not realistic.

Rarely is learning a linear process, and letting kids see how I pivot and deal with the human element of being in learning together each day for a length of time is important. It builds their own confidence in learning as they witness their teacher grapple with similar feelings and experiences in learning. Rather than seeing failure as defeat or stress as a barrier, they begin to see these feelings as mere occurrences that will pop up from time to time in learning. Because they've seen what strategies I've adopted to help work through these situations, students begin to work around them on their own, and the feelings around failure and stress, which all too often are debilitating for our students, suddenly become challenges they can overcome.

As we close this chapter, I want to share an example of authenticity that resonates with my students, from Bill Hader. In a video he created for the Child Mind Institute, titled *What I Would Tell #MyYoungerSelf,* Hader speaks honestly to young people. He talks about his lifelong challenges with anxiety and how he eventually discovered coping strategies to help him manage when these feelings arose.

Scan the QR to watch the video.

I love showing my students this short video. First, Hader is awesomely funny. Kids recognize him from television and movies, so when he begins to speak of his own struggles with crippling anxiety, students are immediately both shocked and engaged. Second, he speaks candidly yet professionally about the matter. He tells us enough detail to hook us, connect with us, and pull us into his subject matter, but he doesn't go too far with the severity of his anxiety. His message provides hope. His message gives clear and achievable strategies. And his tone is personable rather than personal: he connects in a kind and friendly manner without taking the subject matter too far. Have a watch!

#INQUIRYMINDSET IN ACTION

Consider using the "Data We Collect, Data We *should* Collect" image and exercise with your staff and colleagues to brainstorm ways in which you individually build relationships with your students. Curate ideas and speak to the various impacts witnessed through these methods. Identify ways in which your colleagues build relationships that you all agree should be cultural and schoolwide practices in your building. Imagine the benefit of a unified approach to getting to know your students and the broad growth and trust that will occur, from both students and families, as we engage in this commitment together as a staff.

Furthermore, please take some time to reflect on your own inquiry practice and consider how you can have your students' stories, passions, interests, and goals shape your planning, your assessment, and your teaching. As you learn more about your students, how are you becoming a more effective teacher? As you discover their interests and curiosities, how are you making connections to the curriculum *with* them? Document your noticings and observations. Make getting to know your students a formal process in how you spend your time with them. Consider how, as you get to know them, they can get to know each other and themselves better, resulting in a culture of inquiry in the classroom.

PEER AND
SELF-ASSESSMENT

The underpinning value of building relationships with students related to assessment is that they feel psychologically safe in becoming more actively engaged in the process. In asking our students to self-assess with confidence and accuracy, we are asking them to show vulnerability and take risks that they perhaps haven't been asked to do before in their education. In asking students to peer-assess with respect and accuracy, we are asking them to be critical and helpful in shaping someone else's learning. This can be hugely uncomfortable for students. Building strong relationships allows students to self-assess and peer assess accurately. Without strong relationships, any self-assessment and peer assessment that occurs is veiled and tainted by the comparison culture to which our students have become accustomed.

Student agency requires that students feel safe in their learning environment, safe to take risks, to experiment, to be creative, and to be true to themselves.

A CLOSER LOOK AT PEER AND SELF-ASSESSMENT

In my experience, when peer and self-assessment are not useful or beneficial, there is a breakdown in one or more areas:

- Students don't feel psychologically safe to give and receive accurate and helpful feedback.
- A culture of performance dominates the classroom, as opposed to a culture of learning, risk-taking, and of valuing growth over time.
- Students don't know how to give accurate, clear, and helpful feedback that pushes learning forward.
- Not enough time is woven into the learning process consistently, so it never feels like part of the class's routine and practice of everyone in the room.

The behaviours, tasks, routines, and protocols, as they have been scaffolded throughout this book, aim to provide you and your students with the opportunity to make effective change so peer and self-assessment can benefit all who participate in this process. The summation of this scaffolding and the ongoing mindset of inquiring into our learning, our thinking, and ourselves presents us with the language and expertise to maximize assessing together.

Scaffolding, inquiring into our learning, our thinking, and ourselves presents us with the language and expertise to maximize assessing *together*.

Talking about peer and self-assessment through the lens of the Assessment Compass is extremely helpful when it comes to giving agency over learning to students. The Assessment Compass comprises four cardinal assessment directions: accuracy, clarity, fulfillment, and authenticity. These points require our constant refinement, discourse, care, and attention to ensure that our assessment practice is something on which we can rely regardless of the context or situation.

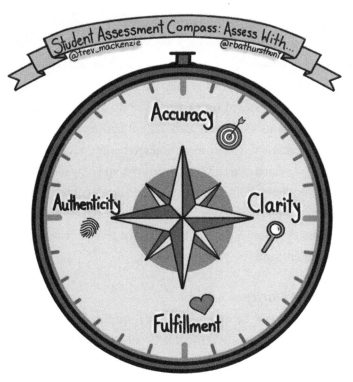

One of the goals I have for my students is that they become such accurate peer and self-assessors that they slowly, over time, become more of an assessment expert themselves. When I share this goal with them, I ask, "Wouldn't it be great if I could back away from assessment entirely because you understand the success criteria with such clarity, and you can assess with such accuracy and meaning, that my role in the assessing is somewhat obsolete?" At first, it may seem like a stretch goal, but with practice and over time, it becomes a reality.

Fine-tuning our Assessment Compass allows us to move toward that vision. Let's look at each of the four cardinal points in more detail:

Assess with Accuracy

We need to actively and consciously be sharing evidence and exemplars of learning, holding them against co-designed success criteria to fine-tune the compass needle toward accuracy. We need to co-design assessment tools so students can gain a deep, clear, and accurate understanding of what they are being assessed on. We need to guide, facilitate, and at times direct the discourse around assessment with students so there is a consistent opportunity for teachers to look for accuracy. When inaccuracy emerges, teachers take the opportunity to clarify, straighten the course, and help all students hit the mark. Students should aim for a close alignment to the teacher's assessment as opposed to an exact match. In my classroom, we often aim for a mark within 5 percent between the teacher assessment, the self-assessment, and the peer assessment.

Assess with Clarity

Students should be able to clearly communicate the details of assessment so that is understandable by all stakeholders in learning.

The clarity should possess curricular rigor, detail, and context. Students need to know the language of the curriculum. Students need to understand the language of the curriculum, and they should use this language as they reflect, as they set goals, and as they plan next steps in learning to determine growth and success. The more clarity teachers can provide, the better. The less ambiguity and uncertainty teachers provide, the better. Learning goals should be shared with students. And because students co-design the success criteria, they should know them. Assessment feedback will be reflected in student-friendly language and provide the opportunity for all students to understand the assessment despite who is doing the assessing, whether it be a teacher or a student as a peer or self-assessor.

Assess for Fulfillment

Assessment should be personally fulfilling, meaningful, and helpful. Students should be able to see themselves in the assessment. Students should be given the opportunity to be assessed from a strength-based perspective, a perspective that allows them to demonstrate their learning, to communicate and engage with others in ways that are equitable and inviting. This process should not be alienating nor should it be divisive or counterproductive. It should be inclusive. This process should be co-designed and leveraged by the partnership between teachers and students. To a certain extent, it should be supported by all members of the learning community as we all actively participate in supporting one another's learning and growth and success. The process is fulfilling in part by the personalized goals students have set throughout the learning process.

Assess for Authenticity

We need to bring authenticity and relevance to the assessment process. Students need to see how the process of learning has tangible and measurable and applicable ties to themselves and the world around them. We need to keep it real: authentic, relevant, and personal for each individual student. This can be done through each student setting personalized goals, reflecting on guiding questions, and being given the opportunity to have a voice in the assessment process. The process of fine-tuning the assessment compass, over time, will result in metacognitive thinking that will be refined to a degree that it transcends content and context. Students will be able to self-assess in a multitude of settings and scenarios because they see the four cardinal points of the assessment compass as being applicable to all facets of life. The active exploration of competencies, dispositions, and habits of mind should be inherently tied to the assessment process and the assessment compass.

Collaborative Assessment Conference

With accuracy, clarity, fulfillment, and authenticity of assessment in mind, I want to share an activity that I find incredibly useful when it comes to fine-tuning the assessment compass of students and giving them an authentic seat at the assessment table—literally. This is accomplished in a collaborative assessment conference.

Teachers and students conferring about learning is a foundational element of the inquiry approach. As you will see in Chapter 11, "Conferring about Learning and Practicing Collaboration," I value the opportunity to sit with students and talk with them about their learning. I outline several processes in that chapter that allow students to prepare for these conferences so they are highly useful, meaningful, and safe conversations. Before we get there, I want to offer a brief example.

In the collaborative assessment conference activity, I sit with a small group of students, three or four at most. I share with them that they will each be doing some of the heavy lifting of learning in this activity and that they will each have an individual responsibility as well as a collective responsibility. I ask for one volunteer in the group to prepare for a conversation about their learning with me in front of their groupmates. I will provide the group with a series of guiding questions for which they will all individually prepare. The volunteer and I have an open discussion stemming from the prompts in which, together, we work our way through their learning, the evidence they have curated to speak to the prompts, and any questions that may surface in our conversation. I give them some time and space to prepare, collaborate, and rehearse.

I let my students know that when it comes time for volunteers to share, I will actively listen for the cardinal points of the assessment compass: accuracy, clarity, fulfillment, and authenticity. These are built into the discussion prompts, and students know they should speak to these points in our collaborative assessment conference.

As our discussion occurs, all group members are encouraged to actively listen and engage in the *thinking* of the conversation. They are encouraged to ask themselves whether they agree or disagree with what surfaces in the open sharing. I also ask them to reflect on the success criteria and learning objectives we have set out for ourselves. Toward the end of the conversation, the group members contribute their personal insights to further the discussion and support the learning of the volunteer as well as the group. As they listen to their groupmates share, keep their own self-assessment in mind, considering whether they are aligned with the conversation that is unfolding before them and whether they are hearing accuracy regarding supporting their own learning.

By having an open conversation with the volunteer, I am able to accomplish a few things:

1. I am able to actively listen and support the speaker. I am able to focus on fine-tuning their assessment compass. I am able

to give them purposeful, helpful, and clear feedback. I am able to best meet their needs in the moment as I respond to and differentiate what they share.

2. I am able to coach and model certain language, reflection, and thinking for the group members that are actively listening. As much as I am supporting the volunteer, I am also supporting the group. I can pause the conversation and make connections to anyone at any given time. Better yet, I can pause the conversation and have the group members make connections at any given time. This frames the collaborative assessment conference to be truly collaborative.

3. I am able to maximize time and effort. I don't need to have the same depth of conversation with each group member. Through their active listening and engagement, my coaching and modeling, as well as my pausing and making connections throughout, each group member is fine-tuning their individual assessment compass as I work with the volunteer.

4. I am able to triangulate assessment. If one student's self-assessment is aligned with what their groupmates share about them, this brings validity to the reflection in a triangulation of data. I am looking for evidence that spans time (not a single occurrence of evidence or a one-off event) and has been witnessed and observed by several members of our learning community.

#INQUIRYMINDSET IN ACTION

Plan for a collaborative assessment experience of your own. Think about a small group of students you feel are perhaps more ready than other to engage in this sort of reflective and open discourse about their learning. Consider the types of questions you will provide students in advance of the conference to help them prepare. What guiding questions could you use in the conference to facilitate the sharing? What prompts can you provide the group members who are listening and supporting their peer? What will the physical space look like? Where will the conference be held? How can you provide some privacy and safety for this first group of volunteers who are demonstrating the bravery to engage in something new and different in their learning experience? Take the time to visualize as much of this exciting opportunity as you can. Your reflections and planning will help make the most of the collaborative assessment conference.

PROCESS OVER
PRODUCT

One question rears its ugly head each year in my classroom. It is inevitable. It surfaces from students, typically when they are asked to engage in thinking and doing. It happens when they are challenged, when they are critically thinking, and when they are making connections. It occurs when they have to share their understanding, curate evidence of their learning, and demonstrate competence. No matter how many times I hear this question, a little bit of my inquiry teacher's heart breaks.

Is this worth marks?

I'm sure you've heard the question before too. No matter how much you've emphasized the importance of learning, of taking risks, of showing vulnerability, and of growth as a process, students have a tough time letting go of the notion that school is about getting good grades.

That's why it's incredibly important that we demonstrate the importance of process over product in our behaviours, tasks, routines, and protocols. If teachers value the importance of process over product, we need to show students we value it through a variety of authentic interactions and processes.

To help illustrate this landscape of process over product, I called on edu-pal Guy Claxton to share with us his vast knowledge and experience in this area.

I have had the pleasure to hear Guy speak on a number of occasions and collaborate with him on a few joined passions of ours. He has written more than thirty books in the field of psychology and education and is the creator of the Learning Power Approach (LPA), a way of teaching that helps students develop into capable and confident learners. The LPA proposes that students can learn *how* to learn and that teachers can teach the skills, knowledge, and processes necessary for students to take ownership of their learning. Guy is a part of the school of thinking I reference in Chapter 4, "The Power of Talk in Assessment," alongside Ron Ritchhart and others (see the Suggested Reading list for more).

In this contribution to *Inquiry Mindset*, Guy examines growth mindset and shares three modes our students put themselves into when they enter the classroom: Learning Mode, Performance Mode, or Defensive Mode. Have a read:

> *Some proponents and popularisers of growth mindset have presented it in unhelpfully "absolutist" terms, as if it were a thing you had, like ginger hair or freckles, that affected all learning everywhere all the time. But a slightly more nuanced and productive way of looking at growth mindset (and fixed mindset) occurred to me a while ago while watching an excellent TED Talk by Eduardo Briceño, an associate of Carol Dweck.*

Here's how I think about it now (which, be warned, is a bit different from the way Eduardo puts it): When students enter a classroom, say, they (usually) unconsciously put their minds into one of a number of different modes. The mode they select determines a range of ways their minds are going to work in that setting. It's like choosing from the menu of sound modes that are built into an amplifier like a television sound bar. You can opt for Drama, Sport, Music, Documentary, and so on. When you make your selection, lots of small adjustments are made inside the amplifier that change the overall quality of the sound.

Just so, kids can set themselves into Learning Mode, Performance Mode, or Defensive Mode. The mode they choose determines how all the different bits of the mind will respond to what happens in that situation.

In Learning Mode, the goal is to enhance long-term competence. Activities involve not-perfect-yet knowledge and skills, things you can improve on. Errors and experimentation are treated not just as normal but as essential. Attention is paid to valuable information and feedback. Cheating is pointless; learning starts from admitting you are not good enough yet at something.

In Performance Mode, by contrast, the goal is to create, as near as you can, flawless performance. Activities are based on already-mastered knowledge and skills. Errors, experimentation, and the appearance of effort are minimised. Attention is on others' assessments of your quality (am I going to get the mark or the applause I want?). Cheating, if you can get away with it, becomes a rational option.

And in Defensive Mode, your sense of self-worth is under attack; your goal is to avoid or neutralise the threat, and to minimise the psychological damage. You are neither learning nor performing; you are surviving. Activities are driven by fight, flight, or freeze. (You try to hide, create a distraction, or seek alternative sources of validation such as peer laughter at your antics.) Attention and energy are dedicated to minimising the damage to self-image and reputation.

The key points that emerge from this way of looking at things are these:

All of these modes are needed at times; they are all valuable.

The issue is this: are our learners in the right one for the current circumstances?

The choice of mode may well depend not on an accurate appraisal of the current situation but on expectations derived from experience in apparently similar situations.

Performance Mode and Defensive Mode are most likely to be selected when mistakes are perceived as being costly, either socially (they will laugh at me) or educationally (I won't get the mark I need).

We as teachers need to send clear signals about whether now is the time for Learning Mode or for Performance Mode and to challenge antiquated or overgeneralised expectations that may be counterproductively flipping our learners into the wrong mode for the occasion.

We also need to be sure that there are no inadvertent cues in our classrooms that are causing students to select an inappropriate or unnecessarily defensive mode.

All other things being equal, we want Learning Mode to be our students' default mode, as this is the mode where learning is fastest and most effective. (That default setting is what we call having a growth mindset.) As soon as the performance

*(or the threat) is over, we and our students should bounce
back into Learning Mode.*

*A fixed mindset is just a way of saying that a student
in our classroom has gotten stuck in Performance Mode
and Defensive Mode; it has become habitual (so we need to
fetch our educational WD40 to free them up to be more agile
and flexible).*

*We can (and should) be explicitly helping our students
to be good at each of the modes: experimental, imaginative,
and adventurous in Learning Mode; well-rehearsed and calm
in Performance Mode; and able to protect, soothe, and take
care of themselves when they find themselves under threat in
Defensive Mode. We also must help them develop the agility
and perception to choose the right mode at the right time.*

I appreciate Guy's way with words and his ability to bring clarity
and sensibility to something we have all experienced and felt in our
classrooms, something that is highly complex (why students behave
in certain ways when it comes to learning), and how we need to find
a balance across all learning modes.

So how do we consistently create the conditions for students to
enter Learning Mode? How do we help them feel at ease and safe
enough to take risks and experiment in their studies and to value
process over product? Let's dive in and find out!

CURATING LEARNING EVIDENCE

I encourage students to document their thinking and learning
in equitable ways, ways that allow them to demonstrate their understanding, display competence, and feel included. It's important that
students know themselves as learners and can identify the strengths
and stretches they bring to the classroom. A deep understanding and

honouring of self give students a successful first step toward curating learning evidence across a span of time.

One of the guiding questions from the Co-Design and Co-Construct chapter was, "If you could show me your learning in any way, how would you show me what you know?" This question is worth revisiting here as we delve into the opportunity of student agency over learning evidence.

Curating learning evidence over time is essential to student-directed learning and assessment. A portfolio of evidence gives them something that they can reflect on, add to, and at some point, share and speak about with their peers and me. The richness and diversity in their curation of learning evidence will support them more powerfully when they experience the next 2 steps of the 10 Steps to Nurture Student Ownership over Assessment: Collaborating and Conferring about Learning and Student Voice in Reporting.

The learning evidence they curate receives feedback from me, feedback from their peers, and a critical review and examination through the lens of a guided self-assessment and reflection activity. Over time students will add to this collection of evidence. As they continue to fine-tune their assessment compasses for accuracy, clarity, fulfillment, and authenticity, they will also learn to identify evidence they would like to put forth to be assessed in a more formal manner.

DON'T GRADE EVERYTHING: STUDENT AGENCY OVER WHAT GETS GRADED

At some point in the learning process, we want to transition students from Learning Mode, in which they take risks and are inventive and creative, to Performance Mode, in which students will select something from their curated learning evidence—something they feel is worthy of examination and grading.

Through a guided reflection process, you can prompt students to reflect on their curated learning evidence, the co-designed assessment tools, and their ongoing peer and self-assessment of their learning evidence to determine which items and evidence they are most proud of.

Below are some guiding questions I ask students to help them decide what should be assessed:

- Where in your curated learning evidence is a demonstration of growth and development over time?
- What is the sample of learning evidence you are most proud of?
- If you were to be graded on one item from all the learning evidence you have curated, on what one item would you like to be graded?
- What piece of learning evidence would you weigh most heavily in your grades? Conversely, what piece of learning evidence would you weigh most lightly in your grades? Why?
- In reflecting on our learning objectives for this unit of inquiry, what evidence would you share that best supports each learning objective?
- In self-assessing using our co-designed rubric, which sample of learning evidence received the most positive feedback or highest grade?
- In sharing your learning evidence with a peer and having them use our co-designed rubric, which sample of learning evidence received the most positive feedback or highest grade?

Whatever surfaces for students through this guided reflection process is what I propose is graded in the unit of inquiry. *Is it for marks?* becomes a question I hear less often from students. As we increasingly focus on Learning Mode and process over product, students gain more agency over what will be graded and what won't. I have witnessed that in this process of sharing ownership over what gets graded, achievement increases, as does student confidence, autonomy, and a sense of fulfillment.

Due-Date Windows

Another way in which I give students agency over the learning process is in a sometimes overlooked yet often stress-inducing characteristic of assessment: due dates.

This activity begins with a powerful conversation I have with students at the start of each year on the topic of wellness. In focusing on building a culture of trust founded on relationship throughout the first weeks of class, I take my time getting into the course. The goal is that we collectively set the stage for successful and equitable learning for all. Part of setting the stage for learning includes providing genuine voice and choice in how our learning community will operate and in what processes we will engage. In my experience, facilitating discourse and supporting students in having responsibility over some of the decision-making in the classroom is a powerful step in creating a culture of learning as opposed to a culture of performance.

I frame this particular discussion by asking the class to tell me about the worries of being a student and any stress that they feel may occur throughout the school year. My intention is to let them know I care about more than their grades; I care about them as people. I want them to know that I care about their emotional and mental health.

The conversation is always lively. I am constantly grateful for the honesty and vulnerability they demonstrate in sharing some of the stresses of being a student. Here's a glimpse into some of what students share:

- We have too much on our plates.
- Sometimes I have a quiz or test every day of the week.
- We are stressed out "to the max."
- Sometimes, if I know there's nothing due in one class, I'll skip that class to study for something I have due in another class.
- I'll always do the work that's worth marks before I do other schoolwork.
- It always seems like there's something due.
- I often have more than three hours of homework a night.
- Teachers encourage us to follow our passions, but then they assign a whole bunch of stuff that takes us away from what we are passionate about.
- School isn't about learning as much as it's about task management.
- Why don't teachers communicate with one another and plan their due dates and test days so they balance out for us?

With these powerful reflections shared and documented, I tell my students that I will commit to doing something about it. I assure them that, together, we can navigate our hectic system because the system itself is not going to change for us.

I then take out a desktop calendar, the old tearaway kind that is used to plan out a month at a glance. Rather than use these on my desk to help me plan out my weeks and month ahead, I hang them on our classroom wall and ask students to help plan our time together with a specific eye on assessments and due dates. I share with them that this will be an ongoing conversation centred around reflection, planning, and sharing.

I provide sticker dots and propose that students stick one on days that they anticipate they will be busy, that they have a quiz or test in another class, that they have an assignment due, or that they just feel will be a stressful time throughout their course load. I promise that I will remind them to reflect and use the collaborative calendars each week so we can all be well aware of what is ahead. We continue to add to the calendars as our weeks unfold and as the tasks and action items from our various individual commitments, both academic and extracurricular, begin to surface.

This is what a few months looks like:

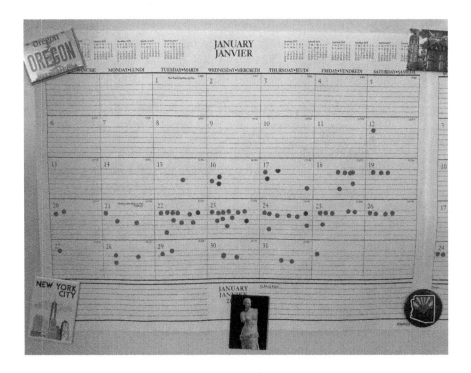

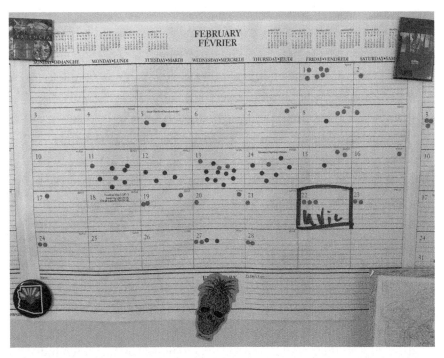

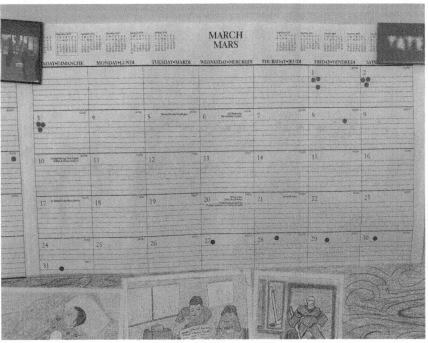

As the weeks unfold, I look for clusters, trends, and any telling signs that students may be feeling overwhelmed. As you can see, the clusters take shape at different times of the year and on different days. Some weeks are busier than others. Some days are more open than others. It appears that most students have different challenges and pressures when it comes to *when* these challenges and pressures arise in their week-to-week workload.

After patterns begin to form, I share with students that our obligation, *together*, will be to plan our work and assessments around the busyness and stress that we see surface in the calendars. As such we adopt *due-date windows* rather than specific, often arbitrary, due dates.

What are due-date windows? Rather than me selecting a due date that meets my needs and marking load, I ask students to turn in their assessments within a span of time, typically a week, that allows them to plan their workflow according to how busy their own individual weeks are. With this flexibility and space, I find that students are better able to plan their process of learning and work getting done, in turn, to better meet their own needs.

This shift has proved transformational. I have witnessed several benefits emerge:

- **My marking load is manageable.Rather than taking in assessments from the entire class in one day, my marking becomes more of a constant trickle throughout the due-date window.** It is something I tackle each day with energy and focus, which allows me to provide clear, purposeful, and timely feedback to each student. I do not experience marking fatigue. My marking is actually more helpful and, in turn, their learning is more greatly impacted.
- **My students appreciate that they can prioritize their studying and workflow.** Some classes do a lot of quizzes

and tests. Some do a lot of project work. Some do a lot of public speaking and presenting. By giving students agency over their due dates in our class, I also give them increased agency of their success across all their classes. They learn to look at *process over product* from a more holistic perspective, one that transcends their learning in a single context or class.

- **We all feel better.** Time and again, students reflect that our class was the least stressful of all of the classes in their schedule. Students share that they are often asked in school about their stress levels and how they are feeling, but rarely is anything done about it. In our class, being asked about their stress actually leads to some changes that impact their well-being. We are able to discuss strategies to manage workload, due dates, task management, and well-being in meaningful and authentic ways.

- **Relationships stay strong.** Allowing agency over due dates results in stronger relationships with my students. By students having the ability to make decisions regarding when they turn in their work, they feel empowered and respected. As such, if a student doesn't meet a due-date window, the conversation about a missing assignment is different. They don't feel hounded, chased, or devalued. They are honest with their reasoning behind the missing assignment and engage in a plan to turn it in as soon as they can. Our relationship is not broken or hardened by an arbitrary assessment policy. The psychological safety and trust that allows us to thrive in Learning Mode remains intact.

I often wedge a weekend in the middle of a due-date window so students have some extended time to dig into their tasks and plan their time accordingly. Time during weeknights can disappear quickly and leave nothing for students who have been asked to build on their learning from the school day. A weekend gives them the opportunity to reflect and plan accordingly.

Student agency—genuine and authentic control over learning—must include genuine and authentic decision-making over the process of learning. I love due-date windows because the genuine and authentic decision-making is over managing their time in a manner that honours their interests, passions, and lives outside of school, and their emotional and mental well-being is given overarching importance.

> Student agency—genuine and authentic control over learning—must include genuine and authentic decision-making over the process of learning.

Another benefit of adopting due-date windows is the opportunity to document, reflect, discuss, and regulate our stress and anxiety. As the year progresses, our collaborative calendars slowly morph into a visual representation of our stress. We begin to see clusters, and trends tend to surface. When we unpack these data, we begin to understand how we can be better prepared for the inevitable stresses that we experience.

- We take notice of which classes or subjects are trending.
- We observe the time of the week, month, term, and semester in which we see patterns.

- We look for clues in the length and duration of particular units of study across student schedules and begin to make predictions as to how these can cause stress and anxiety.
- We consider our individual wellness and discuss our sleep patterns, nutrition, exercise, tech use, and how we are filling our buckets with TLC. We deepen our learning as to how these factors can impact our wellness.

An ongoing conversation about workloads and stress levels allows us to explore ways to self-regulate and manage our well-being. It is not a single, one-off lesson, nor is it disingenuous. The context in which we are learning about self-regulation is directly applicable to their individual experience. It's as though we are exploring a personalized inquiry into their own learning. The outcome provides an individualized road map to specific inquiry skills, learning strategies, and a deeper understanding of how to be successful with greater agency over the process of learning.

#INQUIRYMINDSET IN ACTION

Plan to have an open conversation with your students about process over product. Explore with them what it means to be in Learning Mode or Performance Mode. Help them understand the differences between them and the importance of both. Share with them how you plan to strike a balance in the process of learning throughout your time together as well as a balance between learning and performing. What cues will you use to let them know whether they're in Learning Mode or Performance Mode? What support will you give them so when it's time to perform, they are ready to strut their stuff? Share with them your hopes for their learning and how you aim to support their growth and personal well-being during your time with them.

CONFERRING ABOUT LEARNING AND PRACTICING COLLABORATION

From very early in my career, I believed in the power of timely feedback. I still do, but I've come to a different understanding of what timely feedback means and how I choose to provide it. Let me clarify.

I once believed that timely feedback meant reviewing student work, documenting feedback to accompany this work, and returning it to students *as fast as possible*. Inevitably a piece of this timely feedback consisted of posting student scores, more often than not in the form of a spreadsheet. I believed that students needed to have things wrapped up as quickly as possible: Complete the assignment, turn it in to me, receive feedback and a mark, and move on to the next piece of our curriculum and subsequent assignment. It always felt like there was never enough time and that there was always more we had to do.

Deep learning, embracing reflection, and aiming for growth were nebulous goals and challenging outcomes. I *hoped* these would occur in the midst of the sheer quantity of assignments and assessments we accomplished in class, but the reality is that I was doing more harm than good when it came to helping my students understand themselves better as learners.

Then an incident caused me to change my assessment process. That change has also helped me break down the comparison culture amongst my students. Let me share the story with you.

It was the first block of the day after Christmas break, and the morning bell had just rung. That morning I had arrived at school early so I could print off an updated spreadsheet outlining all the marking I had done over the holiday break. I posted this spreadsheet on a bulletin board outside my classroom, a customary practice of mine, with the aim of keeping my students informed of their progress.

On reflecting on this now, a couple of things strike me: First, the actual message this sent my students on their return to school after the holiday break was not what I intended at all. Certainly, I wanted them to be informed of their progress, but I also wanted them to feel welcomed in coming back and excited for their return to school. I wanted to hear about their holiday, ask them how they'd been, and share with them that I missed them.

Even though I asked them questions that touched on the more humanistic parts of our work as teachers, the moment the students saw the spreadsheet and grades, it was as though their brains switched into Defensive Mode. Adding to that, the public spreadsheet reinforced the comparison culture of assessment I propose we avoid. Immediately after the holiday, students fell into the trap of being identified by a number and comparing their grade with those of their peers.

Sadly, I was the one setting this trap for them. It was my fault! They were given little chance for a fresh start. Rather, a deficit mentality was reinforced from the moment they walked into class. Right away they were given data that made many of them feel as though they weren't *good enough*.

Second, the public posting of their marks, even though the spreadsheet was void of any student names and consisted only of student ID numbers, created an odd social reaction. I was standing at the door of a neighbouring colleague's class as I watched my students from a distance, and I was shocked and saddened by what I witnessed in their behaviour and body language as they found their ID on the spreadsheet. In the few moments before class started that day, I noticed that three groups emerged.

Right away I observed a first group emerge consisting of a few keen and energetic students. These were the high achievers of the class. As soon as they saw the spreadsheet from afar, they excitedly ran to check out their updated grades. These kids smiled and exchanged high fives, literally, seemingly reaffirmed and fulfilled by the assessment feedback. It seemed these were "the winners" of my assessment practice.

Then a second wave of students approached the spreadsheet. These learners were visibly more cautious than the first as they meandered toward the grades with a subtle reluctance and casual uncertainty. They came alone or in pairs (unlike the high achievers who pounced on the spreadsheet in a pack), and they walked calmly, steadily, as they drew nearer the assessment feedback. It was clear that this group was more negatively impacted by what they saw. Some tried to shrug things off, but I could tell that what they were seeing on that report printout didn't feel good. It seemed these were the losers of my assessment practice.

Finally, the third group appeared. The members of this small group hung back, watching from afar, waiting their turn so they could check their updated grades alone. My heart broke. These students were visibly reluctant when it came to checking their mark but savvy in that they waited for complete isolation to do so. They knew where they fell in the assessment pecking order. Sadly, the assessment practice of posting marks publicly had shaped a social dynamic that was unfair, humiliating, and, as I came to realize, completely unnecessary. A few from this group seemed completely disengaged and apathetic. They didn't even bother to look at the spreadsheet, waltzing past it wearing their best "too cool for school" facade. No, this group was the losers of this assessment practice.

Assessment should avoid creating "winners" and "losers." Assessment should guide learning and inform teaching.

Publicly displaying marks did little to inform each student of where they were, where they needed to go next, and what they could do to get there. Numbers on a spreadsheet failed to convey feedback or any semblance of personalized steps toward growth.

Marks are personal. Marks force students to share their vulnerability. Marks can cause a feeling of shame and hurt. I began to ask myself, *how can I keep kids informed and help them improve in their learning whilst avoiding feelings of shame and comparison?*

I've since shifted my assessment practice to include a few simple, informative, and student-centred practices that have transformed how we talk about learning in our classroom.

THE POWER OF CONFERRING WITH STUDENTS

One of the changes I have implemented is to dedicate class time to conferencing with students about their learning. I find this time to be powerfully spent as I get a clear understanding of their needs and can help them stay informed in their learning. Whether it's a quick two-minute check-in, an exit slip briefing, or a more formally prepared conference, the time spent *talking with kids* helps me be the informed and responsive teacher my students need me to be.

Before this one-on-one time, I always share my purpose and intent with the class. I let them know that reflection is powerful in learning and that having one-on-one time with each other is a hallmark of our classroom. I value speaking with them. I value supporting them in a personalized manner. I know that we will both benefit from our conference time. Students excel when they hear you believe in them, and they understand that there's value in what you are jointly committing to. I never miss an opportunity to tell kids I believe in them.

Formal Conferencing

I prefer to hold formally prepared conferences away from the majority of the class so each student and I can have an open and honest discussion about their learning. This aids in breaking down the comparison culture of assessment whilst leveraging the trust and strong relationships we have fostered as a learning community.

By providing some talking points beforehand, I help ease students' anxiety, allowing them to prepare for their sharing. Some of the prompts are task-management focused, some aim to shed light on challenges they may be facing in their inquiry, and some focus on digging into their learning and what they know. I always give them a choice in what they'd like to discuss with me, using either something from my suggestions or something they have personally prepared.

Here is a sampling of the talking points:

- What challenges have you encountered in our inquiry?
- How do you know that the resources you are using for researching are valid and authentic?
- What kind of learning evidence have you been gathering? How is this evidence helpful?
- How has what you know changed since the onset of our inquiry?
- Have you discovered any misconceptions you may have had before our inquiry? How did you discover these misconceptions? What changed your thinking?
- Are you on task to be successful in our inquiry?
- What strategies have you been using to help you be successful in our inquiry?
- What aha moments have you experienced in our inquiry?
- What have you been proudest of in these past days or weeks? Why?
- Do you have any questions for me?
- How can I better support you?
- Have you been given enough time to work toward your task? Have you been given enough support to complete your task?
- What could we be doing differently to ensure you are successful in our inquiry?

In my experience, students appreciate these prompts. They enjoy being in charge of the chat and having choice in what they'll bring to the conference. They also feel a sense of trust and safety because they know we can openly discuss the support they need. Agency over assessment can be challenging for many students. Having this conference in a safe space, in terms of being physically removed from others as well as in my acceptance and honouring of their experience, is required to leverage the potential in conferencing. Providing them one-on-one time to discuss their thinking, the challenges they're facing, and strategies to move forward is always better received in the safety of a conference.

I also use a handful of responses to help create a thread of empathy between my students and me. The stress and anxiety that all too often rear their ugly heads during learning demand a heartfelt and welcoming response from the teacher, one that models compassion and demonstrates how, together, we can overcome moments when big feelings may well up.

I have found that students are more open to revealing these feelings within the safety of a one-on-one conference. I have also found that how I respond to student stress, anxiety, concern, or worry has a direct impact on their feelings and how they view the outcome of their feelings. I am continually working toward improving in this area of gentle, flexible, and responsive discourse.

The following responses have helped me in this endeavour. Consider them for yourselves. When working with a student who is feeling overwhelmed in inquiry, I might reply:

- *It's normal to have these feelings.* As an adult, my ability to navigate my circumstances, not by what I encounter, but by how I approach it, models a level of resiliency I want all of my students to achieve. This statement helps normalize what students are experiencing. Letting my students know that their feelings are somewhat universally experienced grants us access to a greater network of support and acceptance.

- **What would work for you here?** This is a significant invitation for joint problem solving. Having encountered similar experiences many times throughout my career, I am well versed in offering strategies to overcome challenges. By beginning with student voice and encouraging them to reflect and identify probable solutions, we are moving away from helicopter teaching—the tendency to overprotect and direct our students when they face challenges—and toward fostering agency with our guidance and support.

- **What is your plan moving forward?** I try to conclude conferences by encouraging students to act on their ideas and needs. This question does two magical things. First, it proposes self-reflection on what we've discussed and taking a personalized inventory of everything we've unearthed together. Second, it shifts our eyes to the future and what the student's next steps could be, using the strategies and awareness gleaned from the conference. Looking toward possibility helps to build great confidence in the student. Time and again I witness confidence personified: shoulders back, eyes up, gusto for the future.

I always leave these conferences with a deeper understanding of my students as well as a heightened appreciation for the time we spend conferencing. These are some of the most humane interactions we have together. They shape our next steps and allow us to make informed plans on what we need to do to move forward in our inquiry.

Conferring with students about learning will provide some of the most meaningful interactions in the inquiry classroom.

Timing these talks is an important planning decision to consider. I typically provide ten-minute time slots for each student and hold conferences for as long as necessary. Some students require less conference time than we planned for. Some require more conference time than the allotted ten minutes. Structuring in some space for agility and responsiveness is helpful to ensure every student gets the time they need and leaves feeling heard, supported, and clear on how to move forward.

While I am meeting with students one-on-one, the rest of the class prepares for their conference using the prompts I have provided. They may be rehearsing in pairs how their conference might go, role playing as both the student and teacher. This is helpful in that it provides some thinking from the perspective of being the teacher, listener, and supporter. Swapping hats, so to speak, gives them the opportunity to share strategies and advice with their peers. Some students choose to quietly plan for their conference, gathering evidence they'd like to discuss in our time together. Those students who have met with me begin working on whatever next steps we outlined during the conference. Rarely do I encounter a time when I am conferencing in which students are not on task.

Have a look at this insight from inquiry friend Kath Murdoch as she further develops the role and power of conferencing with our learners:

Of the myriad of approaches to assessment in the inquiry classroom, conferring with individuals would top my list. Of course, teachers regularly converse with students, but true conferring brings both an intention and attention to a conversation that elevates it well above a quick check-in or informal chat. A conference is a planned, purposeful routine to which teachers and students come prepared. Although they are most often quite short (an effective conference can last as little as five minutes), clear structures and expectations help maximise the benefits for both teacher and student.

Pioneered by the work of Donald Graves in the 1980s and continued in more recent times by numerous literacy educators including Carl Anderson and Debbie Miller, conferring with learners has most often been associated with writing and reading workshops. The technique, however, can be applied to any learning context and aligns beautifully with the principles underpinning inquiry.

Skilled conferring provides powerful insights into students' thinking and allows us to listen in ways less possible when working with groups. These interactions help us slow down and pay close attention which, in turn, enables careful, just-in-time feedback and targeted teaching points. A good conference means we are noticing and responding in the moment and giving our full attention to the learner, thereby communicating an important message: I value you, I value your thinking and learning, and I am here for you. *Bringing routine conferences into our repertoire nurtures relationships which, in turn, helps learners feel safe to share their questions, uncertainties and struggles, thus widening the window we have into their thinking.*

Effective conferring requires an inquiry mindset. We approach the conversation with curiosity and an open mind, using questions that invite the learner to talk about where they are currently at with their learning. It might be as simple as, Can you tell me about what you are working on? What are you most happy with? What are you finding challenging? Say more about that. *Listening is the most important element of this time. When we take the time to truly sit with each student, we begin to notice things that no test, exam or summative task will reveal. What students choose to share, their body language, tone, and expression, coupled with the artefacts they bring to the conference, all provide a powerful opportunity for us to gain a deeper insight into the story beyond the task itself.*

Skilled conferring demands we be completely present to the learners' offerings and simultaneously notice what they are revealing and the implications for next steps. Above all, conferring should be an empowering process for the learner. Teachers learn to ask questions that result in what Dan Rothstein describes as the "lightbulb effect." The teacher, as inquirer, uses questions and probes to prompt the learner to rethink, stretch, or change direction. This does not preclude the teacher from offering suggestions or using the conference to model, demonstrate, or explain. The key is to limit teaching points to one or two—to keep the conference targeted, short, and supportive with the locus of control remaining firmly with the student.

The idea of regular, focussed conferring with individuals may seem at odds with the frantic pace of the typical classroom. There is no doubt it requires clear, organised routines and systems for those who are in conference as well as those continuing with independent learning. But it is worth the effort. When combined with solid documentation, strong intention, and an open, inquiring mindset, conferring is a beautiful vehicle for assessment as, for, and of learning.

Two-Minute Checks

A short and snappy reflection activity is a quick way to get a sense of what students are thinking. Think of it as a mini conference that is more student directed. With our chairs we create two large circles—one inside the other—so we can sit face-to-face. I provide a reflection prompt and call on students to role play as the speaker and the listener. I either sit outside the circles or wander around the room listening to the discussions, giving two minutes for students to share and chat.

Once the time has passed, I ask students to show me with their fingers how many more minutes they need to finish up. I try to provide some flexibility so their time together is fruitful. I then pause and ask students if they'd like to share any advice they received that they believe was helpful. I may also chime in with something I heard that I think others would benefit from hearing as well.

Throughout the activity, I am actively observing and listening to what students are sharing. I try to gain whatever evidence I can glean from their conversations. I use these observations to guide next steps and plans together.

I take into account the following considerations when planning for conferencing:

- When is a more formally prepared discussion needed?
- Do all of my students need to have a chat or conference?
- How can I best prepare students for conferencing?

Holding up a Conversation in Class

I often pause class to "hold up a conversation," a phrase my students have become accustomed to and now respond accordingly. Holding up a conversation is an intentional response to a talk with an individual student.

Some of the most powerful mentoring and student-directed problem-solving occurs when you least expect it. Often it happens during the informal interactions and talks throughout a lesson, when time and space has been provided for kids to dig into their learning. Time and again, after I have made several trips through the classroom aiming to support students in their learning, the very moment I sit down, I am often approached by a student for support. I believe there is something about the safety in coming to a table or desk away from their peers that allows students to share a challenge or ask a question that they didn't quite feel comfortable enough to explore within earshot of their peers. It's in these moments that I use the holding up a conversation strategy.

In listening to a student's needs and helping them troubleshoot a challenge or barrier they are encountering in their learning, I may discover that our little, informal chat is one that could benefit others. I ask the student whether they would mind me sharing some of our conversation with the larger group. In doing so, they agree to share their vulnerability with others, a direct result of the strong relationship we have built and the trust we have fostered. I then pause the class and gather their attention, announcing that I would like to "hold up a conversation."

This announcement is a cue for the class to focus on what is being shared and question how they can learn from the conversation that is about to be modeled. Once I have their attention, the individual student and I revisit our conversation, reenacting what we discussed and the conclusions at which we arrived. Together we model problem-solving and the powerful discourse of reflection and subsequent action we experienced.

The student who has volunteered to hold up their conversation with me often responds confidently to the public display of problem solving and role playing, because they have worked through the challenge with me and now possess a solution or plan to help them move forward. Their display of pride and confidence inspires other students to come up and share their own respective challenges. Furthermore, the strategies or solutions we share in our reenactment often help others in their own learning. I have found that if one student is experiencing something challenging, it is likely that others are experiencing a similar challenge. Raising students' voices and honouring their experiences creates empathy and equips learners with the tools of resiliency and growth mindset.

DOING COLLABORATION RIGHT

One of the most important competencies we can nurture in today's inquiry classroom is that of collaboration. Working together and understanding the depth and nuance needed to coordinate with others is an immensely important skill. Take a look at any "Skills You Need to Succeed in Today's Workplace" article or ask anyone in a position of management or leadership, and you're certain to hear an emphatic retelling of the same notion: collaboration matters. With our support, guidance, and coaching, students benefit greatly from the immense power that comes with collaboration. Collaboration, when done right in schools, can lead to amazing outcomes:

- The ability to actively listen and understand what others are contributing
- The recognition of one's strengths and what each team member brings to the collective direction
- The ability to lead and, simultaneously, to be led
- The ability to put yourself into the shoes of another, to truly feel and have empathy
- The sheer joy experienced through the social interaction of working together. Forming friendships is fun!

Despite these clear and plentiful benefits, year after year, I work with students who are reluctant to lean in when it comes to group work.

In my experience, the reluctance for collaboration is due, in part, to how we assess learning in a collaborative setting. As we know, assessment can cause anxiety, stress, and a negative and misinformed understanding of self. When working in a group setting, the chance of an unjust mark being given to a student is quite high. I always remind myself that when it comes to assessment and collaboration, I need to ensure I am not assessing a behaviour. If a student is shy or introverted, is a mark for the strength of their collaboration unfair? Absolutely.

This creates a challenging assessment dilemma: How can I teach collaboration yet not have it negatively impact a student's wellness or their mark in class? How can I create conditions that encourage risk-taking so students become stronger collaborators? How can I honour all students in my classroom, both my extroverts and leaders and my shy and introverted learners?

With these questions in mind, I work to scaffold our collaboration so that students gain confidence whilst garnering the skills and understandings needed to be successful when working with others. I do this in a number of ways. Let's look more closely at a few of them.

TOSS THE SEATING PLAN

One way I promote trust and collaboration in the classroom is by giving students a choice in whom they would like to sit with. I tossed out the seating plan long ago in favour of student choice. This is one more way I provide agency over decision-making. It creates autonomy and fosters responsibility.

Learning can be fun and engaging when it is social. As such, I want students to have a social experience in our classroom. Whether it is through collaboration, teamwork, talking, or discussion, learning thrives in the inquiry classroom when it can be built on social constructivism.

I appreciate that shy, introverted students want to sit with other shy, introverted students. Why? Because they share a common experience. They have empathy for one another. They know what their groupmates are feeling because they often feel it too. It is in this shared experience that trust is formed, allowing group members to be honest in their collaboration and support each other in ways that are difficult in other group compositions.

I feel the same way when English Language Learner (ELL) students sit with other ELL students. The skills and strategies ELL students use to be successful in class are often similar no matter their first language. Whether it's using Google Translate, consulting a picture dictionary, or speaking or writing in their first language before translating their writing into English, I appreciate that by giving students agency over choosing whom they would like to sit with, I am also giving them agency over being successful in a highly personalized manner.

Providing agency over seating arrangements also allows me to differentiate within learning more effectively. I can easily wander through the room, from group to group, and observe students as they share, discuss, and work together, all the while considering how I can better meet their needs in the moment. This sort of timely responsiveness provides personalized support so students feel comfortable and confident in collaboration; for example, a group of ELL students might require similar strategies of support. I can easily sit with them in inquiry as we work together to discuss and move forward in their learning.

Collaboration is also supported by the design of our space. The start of our lessons typically begins with our classroom arranged in short rows of three desks each. All the desks face one of the whiteboards and the projector screen in the room. It's very common, however, for me to ask students to "turn and face," a request for them to turn their desks in toward their group so they form a small pod of three, an ideal structure for collaboration.

Discover Personal Relevance in Collaboration

To prepare and empower students for collaboration so their time working together is meaningful as well as successful, we must spend time digging into the qualities of powerful collaborators. Consider questions such as, *What do collaborators do? What does strong group work look like? What skills help when it comes to teamwork?* Discuss these questions with your students and gather your thinking in a collective brainstorm on a whiteboard or in a Google Doc. This is another great example of co-designing with students, as outlined in Chapter 3, "Co-Design and Co-Construct."

Here's a sample from a conversation that occurred with students in my classroom:

We believe that collaborators are . . .

- Active listeners
- Focused
- Kind and generous
- Prepared
- Curious
- Adaptable
- Organized
- Friendly
- Possessors of a strong work ethic
- Appreciative

- Empathetic
- Team focused: "we before me"
- Able to make connections
- Able to build and value relationships
- Diplomatic
- Able to self-regulate

To equip students to become better collaborators, we begin with some reflection. Considering the traits we have identified as well as a list of powerful skills for collaboration that I add to our brainstorm activity, I ask them to reflect on how strong of a collaborator they are. Using a simple four-point identifying scale (3 = I do it really well; 2 = I do it some of the time; 1 = I know I need to work on this; 0 = I don't possess it at all), each student records a personal inventory from our list of skills of a strong collaborator.

A student's reflection may look like this:

- Active listener—3
- Focused—3
- Kind and generous—2
- Prepared—1
- Curious—1
- Adaptable—2
- Organized—1
- Friendly—3
- Strong work ethic—1
- Appreciative—3
- Empathetic—3
- Team focused, "we before me"—2
- Makes connections—2
- Builds and values relationships—3
- Diplomatic—3
- Can self-regulate—3

When students have completed their personal inventory of collaboration skills, I ask them to identify two strengths they feel are their most powerful groups skills as well as two areas they would like to improve over the coming weeks of our inquiry. We then create groups based on these specific characteristics. I prompt students to find a group that balances one another's strengths and goals; for example, a group cannot consist of students who have all self-assessed a lower number when it comes to organization. Any student who has self-assessed low with this skill needs to find a partner that has self-assessed high in this skill. I then prompt them to create their own groups with this information and balance in mind.

The ensuing discourse and sharing of one another's inventory information is amazing to witness. They personalize the group composition to an extent that is relevant to them, on a level that is aligned to an individualized goal and tied to a desire to genuinely improve as a collaborator. Time and again, students tell me they feel this process of choosing a group is relevant because it removes the often-arbitrary decision made by a teacher and puts the responsibility and onus on the student. They value identifying a goal—one that is tied to a competency standard as opposed to a content standard—and working toward honing the skills they have set for themselves.

Many schools, districts, and organizations have mandated collaboration to be taught and assessed as part of their curriculum. This is nothing new. ISTE standards, the International Baccalaureate (Primary Years Programme, Middle Years Programme, Diploma Programma), 21st Century Skills, the College, Career, and Civic Life (C3) Framework for Social Studies Standards, and the Next Generation Science Standards are all examples of curricula and frameworks that highlight the importance of collaboration. I would wager that, somewhere in your own curriculum, collaboration is highlighted as well. In inquiry I focus on how I can provide personal relevance and meaning to every student when it comes to exploring such curricula *together*. This exercise outlines, with collaboration as our lens, how the balance between personal relevance and exploring the prescribed objectives of our curriculum can be accomplished.

With groups formed and strengths and goals identified, we begin our collaboration and inquiry with a greater sense of community and heightened personal relevance. During the coming weeks and throughout learning, I will do several things to ensure students continue to keep these goals in mind and work toward a personally successful outcome.

First, we pause and reflect throughout inquiry to help students understand how things are developing when it comes to meeting their goals. I ask students to describe a recent circumstance where they knew they were using their goal skills to help in collaboration or to reflect on the past week and identify a strategy they used to aid them in meeting their goal. The opportunity to pause in learning and reflect is critical to this process of personalized growth. Whether it's with a turn-and-talk exercise, asking them to record their reflections as a journal entry, or in a one-on-one conference with me, students value the chance to reflect, see growth, and plan their next steps.

Second, I conduct mini-lessons on the goals students have set for themselves to provide them with the knowledge, strategies, and resources to help them be successful. These mini-lessons are a lot of fun! They are typically ten to fifteen minutes in duration and cater to a small group of students who all share a particular goal. I might, for example, call on students who have identified organization as their goal. At a round table, we may watch and discuss short TED Talks, analyze an infographic, read an article, or share a reflection from one another all on the topic of organization. I may share a few organizational strategies I personally use or have observed other students using. I may even ask this small group to share what they have learned from their collaboration in watching how their peers organize themselves. Students love these mini-lessons because they are highly relevant, engaging, and helpful. I enjoy them because the groups are small, the lessons are short, and I know they have an immediate impact on student growth.

Finally, I always include a student reflection and self-assessment as part of the assessment process. With student voice woven into the planning, organizing, and assessment process throughout the unit of inquiry, it should be included here as well. Students value the chance to have one final reflection regarding their goal. They also appreciate the opportunity to self-assess to determine how well they did in meeting their goal. The strength of each student's collaboration, therefore, isn't tied to a mandated rubric or assessment criteria. Rather, it is built by their own personal reflection and experience in collaboration. This personalisation is incredibly powerful for students. It helps develop confidence and authenticity in self-assessment whilst building student agency and ownership over the assessment process in inquiry.

#INQUIRYMINDSET IN ACTION

Spending time in class talking with students one-on-one about their learning is a worthwhile investment. Facilitating talk amongst students as they confer about their learning is equally powerful. When it comes to conferring with your students in a one-on-one setting, what roadblocks or procedural challenges do you anticipate may arise? When it comes to students conferring together, in pairs or small groups, what roadblocks or procedural challenges do you anticipate may arise? Having this in mind before you implement these opportunities to confer will have the sharing be natural, uninhibited, and successful.

THE POWER OF
STUDENT VOICE
IN REPORTING

The culminating step of the assessment continuum is to infuse more student voice into the formal assessment and reporting processes of our schools, specifically when it comes to report cards. The steps outlined in this book, the behaviours and decisions, the structures and processes, and the mindset of agency and cultivating accurate and confident assessment experts in the room has brought us to a space where we can leverage this opportunity.

We can now sit with students, confer with them about their learning, examine their body of work and the evidence they have gathered, and together we can write report cards that are rich in authentic student voice.

Report cards that are co-constructed with students allows us to close the agency loop in a meaningful and authentic way.

I have been doing this sort of assessment conference for several years, and it has provided a much more meaningful and informative reporting experience for students and parents as well as for me. It has saved me time, effort, and energy, and I have witnessed that students have gained a clearer path to growth and success for the oncoming term after the activity.

Before we begin to unpack this co-constructed report card writing process, let's look at a few of the benefits your students have achieved, assuming they traveled the assessment continuum outlined in this book:

- **You are both used to co-designing and sharing the heaving lifting of learning.** Your students are now accustomed to taking on some of the responsibilities of the classroom. They are comfortable sharing their voice to shape a process and an outcome. You have been partners in learning for some time, and this powerful partnership now extends to this conference.
- **You are both used to leveraging thinking routines and reflection.** Your students are now accustomed to being critical about their thinking. They know how to analyse and make connections across their learning because you have been coaching and modeling these skills. This reflection and the thinking routines will now shape this conference.

- **You are both used to setting personalized goals and planning the process to work toward these goals.** Your students are accustomed to reflecting on these goals, writing about them, documenting their growth and the challenges they encountered, and curating evidence of their learning throughout the year. This process will guide the discussion in this conference.
- **You are both familiar with using questions to shape learning.** Your students have explored questions at a conceptual level. They have thrived in responding to your guiding questions, and these guiding questions have led to students having more agency over their learning. Guiding questions will now shape this conference.
- **You are both used to using feedback to dig into learning and plan next steps.** Your students value learning as a process that requires feedback to determine next steps. They understand that the learning isn't in the mark or a grade or a percentage. The learning is in the process, and feedback guides the process. The feedback from throughout the year will now shape this conference.
- **You are both used to the strong trust and honesty and vulnerability that have been shaped through the nurturing of relationships in the classroom.** Your students have sharpened their assessment skills under your guidance, coaching, and modeling. They can now self-assess with accuracy, detail, and confidence. Their assessment compass is aligned and ready to guide them in this conference.
- **You are both used to discussing process over product.** Your students have been gathering evidence of learning throughout your time together. They have curated highlights of their learning (items they're proud of) as well as evidence

of challenges they have encountered. They have at the ready the good, the bad, and the ugly of their learning, and they will use these to discuss their learning in this conference.

- **You are both used to conferring about learning.** Students are accustomed to sitting with you and talking about their thinking, reflecting on your feedback and feedback from their peers, unpacking guiding questions, and using talk as an assessment method. Talking and conferring will now bring everything together.

In reflecting on these benefits that your students will have achieved throughout this assessment continuum, when you feel your students are ready for this conversation, please proceed. If they have confidently taken on this agency and understanding of assessment with accuracy, meaning, and purpose, then they, and you, are ready for this rich opportunity.

It is important that you take a more active role in this conference for those students who are not quite prepared with assessment accuracy and agency. If this is the case, don't rob these students of the experience to confer in this highly meaningful manner. Rather, please take on a bit more of the heavy lifting of the conference. Guide more. Lead more. Share more. Just because some students are not ready now does not mean they won't be ready one day. The seeds you have planted will eventually grow. An arbitrary report card timeline does not gauge student success in taking on agency nor your success in scaffolding toward more agency over assessment.

Now, allow me to describe the process of writing report cards *with* students.

At the end of a reporting period, I create a Google Form for my students to begin to reflect on the learning objectives from our course. I simply copy and paste these learning objectives right from our curricular documents and revise a few into more student-friendly language.

Here are some examples from the form:

- I can access information for diverse purposes and from a variety of sources to inform writing.
- I can think critically, creatively, and reflectively to explore ideas within, between, and beyond texts.
- I can respectfully exchange ideas and viewpoints from diverse perspectives to build shared understanding and extend thinking.
- I can demonstrate speaking and listening skills in a variety of formal and informal contexts for a range of purposes.
- I can recognize the complexities of digital citizenship.
- Share one thing you'd like to draw my attention to that is powerful evidence of your learning.

I then propose our report card writing process to students. I share with them that they will use the assessment skills they have acquired throughout the year in this conversation and that they will prepare the following for an assessment conference with me. My directions for students look like this:

- Please complete the self-assessment Google Form.
- Reflect on a few key competencies of our course (as seen in the Co-Design and Co-construct chapter).
- Please prepare to discuss the following guiding questions: who are you becoming as a learner? What are you noticing about yourself? What do you want to develop over time?
- Identify the strengths and stretches that you bring to their own learning.
- Narrow your focus on a future learning goal for the coming term.

- Attach a strategy that you can use to help meet your future learning goal.
- Use a thinking routine to discuss some of your learning goals (for example, the "I Used to Think, Now I Think" routine outlined in Chapter 4, "The Power of Talk in Assessment").
- Reflect on your body of work from the term and, in doing so, identify a grade that you feel reflects this body of work.
- Spend a bit of time rehearsing for our assessment conference.

I follow the process described in the *Formal Conferencing* section in Chapter 11, "Conferring About Learning and Practicing Collaboration." To review:

- Meetings are held one-on-one, away from peers for privacy, honesty, and trust.
- Reflection prompts help students by providing direction and some talking points for our conference.
- Having a few responses at the ready to create empathy, understanding, and support from the teacher to the student are incredibly helpful.
- Plan for ten-minute time slots for each student and hold conferences for as long as necessary. Some students require less conference time, some require more. Be prepared to be flexible.
- While students await their turn, they can be doing several things: preparing for their conference using the prompts, rehearsing in pairs how their conference might go, quietly gathering evidence they'd like to discuss in our time together. Those students who have met with you may begin working on whatever next steps you outlined together during the conference.

I begin each conference by asking students to speak to their self-assessment and to the prompts they prepared. I ask for them to share a future learning goal for the coming term (or future studies if our time together is coming to a close) as well as a strategy to help support them in meeting this goal. Using my laptop computer, I type their reflection into the report card comment section, directly into the reporting system our specific school district uses. This is done *as they talk.* I may ask them to repeat things they said or to elaborate on an idea to provide more detail for the report. I may hear something that provides us an opportunity to unpack it more meaningfully together and shape the report in a way that is more robust, authentic, and helpful. I then read the comment back to them and ask them for their approval. If revisions are required, we make them together. If they approve, we move on.

Time and again, this process is positive and meaningful for all parties involved. Students tend to glow when they hear the words that will be on their report card—words that their parents will soon read. Here's a sample:

> *A strong collaborator who does well in small groups, Jackson perfectly shares the workload with others and specifically enjoys working with a friend. A self-identified strength is his communication with others. Jackson always seeks out clarification from Mr. MacKenzie and his peers. He enjoys receiving and giving feedback to improve and broaden his perspective. Work ethic is another area of strength for Jackson. He is on-task and does his work in a timely manner. A future learning goal is to improve his essay writing. A strategy to help in this area is to use a peer edit to revise his work.*

We conclude our conference by reviewing their body of work from the entire term and coming to a grade *together.* Students bring assignments and artifacts that they would like to share and speak to in our conference. I ask them to begin with an artifact that they are most proud of, that highlights their strengths and potential in the course. Next, I ask them to speak to evidence from their learning that demonstrates growth over time. This could be something that illustrates a deeper understanding being formed, refinement of a skill being accomplished, or a series of challenges that they faced and subsequently overcame. This is more from *the bad and the ugly* side of their curated evidence.

It should be noted that throughout the year, I have documented marks through the process of providing helpful formative feedback. These marks reflect an array of diverse summative assessments and include students voice and choice in sharing their learning as we co-designed and leveraged agency together. We have now arrived at a time when students can speak to this collection of marks, their curated evidence of learning, and their highlights and growth throughout the year. They can speak to things they are most proud of and the personalized growth they made over our time together. These conversations help nullify the sometimes arbitrary and dehumanizing weight of certain assignments over others. They put my students and me in a position where we can talk through their body of work together as opposed to merely entering a bunch of numbers into a reporting system for it to average out scores. I have an averaged score in my gradebook, but through the process of our conference we will come to an agreed-on mark together.

Let me provide you with an assessment scenario where this conversation would be helpful. Over the course of several weeks, I have five summative assessments recorded and entered in my gradebook, all of which have an equal value and weighting:

Student 1 Scores	Student 2 Scores
Assignment 1: 8/10	Assignment 1: 3/10
Assignment 2: 9/10	Assignment 2: 5/10
Assignment 3: 8.5/10	Assignment 3: 7/10
Assignment 4: 9/10	Assignment 4: 8.5/10
Assignment 5: 10/10	Assignment 5: 9/10
Average: 44.5/50	Average: 32.5/50
Percentage: 89%	Percentage: 65%

Consider a few questions:

- Which student was successful right away in the assessment process?
- Which student was consistently successful throughout the assessment process?
- Which student demonstrated more growth and resilience throughout the assessment process?
- Which student likely responded to feedback to make progress over time throughout the assessment process?

The whole story of Student 2's learning is not told by the collection of data alone. I do not believe it fair or equitable to simply average out a series of data points to determine their final mark. Their learning evidence, the curated samples of their growth, the challenges they faced, and the student's story and experience allow us to gain a much clearer and accurate picture of their learning over time. It's through assessment conferences that we can surface this helpful information and have it guide learning and shape the formal assessment process.

I have consistently noticed that the self-assessment students share and the mark they have selected is aligned with my assessment. As we have become partners in assessment and students have grown into assessment experts of their own right, these conferences reveal accuracy and ownership over their learning in a way that we can leverage in these formal conferences. That is so powerful!

At times I encounter students who have underassessed, feeling that their mark is lower than what I have recorded for them. I have witnessed that students can tend to undervalue their growth and undervalue the highlights of their learning. These conversations, when they arise, are great opportunities to let students know that I believe a higher mark is warranted as I speak to their body of work, the growth I have witnessed, and the evidence they have gathered. As you recall from the *Assessment Tools* section of Chapter 3, "Co-Design and Co-Construct," I often use exemplars to sharpen assessment accuracy. If a student undervalues their learning in this conference, I refer to some exemplars in our conversation. We may even unpack a few samples of student learning that will help provide some direction for us to move forward.

Rarely do I encounter students who have overassessed their mark. If this occurs, I go through the same process outlined in the above scenario:

- Review the body of work together.
- Share the growth I have witnessed.
- Review the evidence they have gathered.
- Use the exemplars to shape the assessment conversation.

Some of the added benefits I have witnessed from this process, from both my perspective and that of my students, include the following:

- Students appreciate that their self-assessment actually impacts their mark and that it is not merely an activity they participate in. They understand the grade we eventually agreed on to a deeper degree.

- Students appreciate that they have clarity in their grade, and we had a conversation about learning rather than just a number or percentage being weighed and created by the reporting software. They feel as though this created a sense of ownership over their mark.
- Students feel like they had a better understanding of their learning and how to improve in the future. They enjoy setting a personal learning goal as opposed to being told they aren't good at something.
- From the students who underassessed, hearing that I believed their mark should be higher made them feel confident and valued.
- Students appreciate leading the conference and sharing particular details about their learning that they wanted to have shape their assessment. Students feel like this allows me to get to know them better.

From my experience over the past several years of using this process with students, I have been exceptionally pleased with their response to and growth from the process. Note that my students do not grade grub, overassess, or overadvocate for a mark. They do not pick their own grade. The conference is a conversation about their body of work, looking at the assessments (both formative and summative) from our time together, and students state a mark they feel was warranted. We work from this self-assessment to determine their grade *together*.

#INQUIRYMINDSET IN ACTION

At the onset of this chapter, I reviewed the nine previous steps of the assessment continuum and asked you to reflect on your students' ability to accurately, meaningfully, and confidently co-construct report cards. Before you begin this process with your students, take some time to reflect on each one of your students. For those who are ready for the conversation, how could you elevate their experience and have it be fulfilling and meaningful for each of them? For those who are perhaps not as ready for the conversation, what scaffolding could you use to better meet their needs? What guiding questions could you ask to support them in the process of talking about their learning? What learning evidence would you like to surface in your assessment conference with each of these students?

SECTION 3

CREATE ASSESSMENT ALIGNMENT AND CAPACITY SCHOOL–WIDE

One common barrier I have observed to successful implementation in education of any sort, whether it be inquiry, curriculum planning, or in our case, assessment, is a lack of consistent approaches and practices across a school. Ensuring every stakeholder is talking about teaching and learning using similar language is critical. But actually putting this language into practice with some semblance of consistency so that behaviours, responses, and decisions become somewhat expected or predictable is incredibly tricky.

Let me give you an example.

One measure I use to determine whether there is equitable assessment across a school is sorting out whether all students have a similar chance of success regardless of who their teacher is. Students in the same course taught by two different teachers should, to a certain degree, learn the same skills, have access to the same books and technology, explore the same styles of writing, receive similar support, and even explore the same methods of formative and summative assessments. As I walk through the halls of the schools I support, I look into classrooms to see whether students have a similar chance of success and are similarly prepared for their next step in their learning. If I observe inconsistencies, I put my inquirer hat on and dig into what's happening that could explain the inequity I am witnessing.

When inequity is the case, I often discover a lack of alignment in how we communicate with students about assessment and how we prioritize, weigh, and categorize our assessment practice. One rich example I can provide is demonstrated in how teachers across a specific grade value homework differently than their colleagues teaching the exact same course in the exact same grade. I often observe that certain teachers have hard deadlines and penalties for homework, and others accept homework late with no penalty at all. Some give marks for effort or completion with no regard to whether the homework was done with any degree of quality, care, or whether it is even correct.

This inconsistency is problematic for our students. And to be clear, I value homework and the impact extra study outside of school can have on learning and achievement. I do not, however, believe homework should be used as an assessment, be considered an indicator of achievement, or have an impact on a student's mark.

On one hand, some students have extracurricular activities that they have committed themselves to, interests and passions that take up much of their time outside of school, that pull them away from doing their homework. On the other hand, some of our students have more important things to worry about than homework. Whether it be poverty, addiction, abuse, or trauma, many of our students are focused on love and survival, not an assignment or a test or homework that's been given.

The landscape of how our students spend time outside of school is vastly diverse. Some homes have parents that sit with their children and help them with their homework. Some of our students don't have homes. Putting a mark on homework that shapes a student's grade reinforces the assessment inequity we are trying to avoid.

Thus, when we have teachers who value and assess homework so differently, in the same school, at the same grade level, even teaching the same curriculum, our students suffer. Whether it be hard deadlines and penalties for homework, flexibility in accepting homework late without penalty, or giving marks for homework based on effort and completion, the inconsistency in how we assess causes confusion, chaos, and even a crisis of identity for the students with whom we work.

Students are trying their best to understand the language of assessment and apply it to their own learning. Reflection, formative feedback, summative assessment, homework, tests, marks versus grades, and even process and outcome are all examples of assessment jargon that we introduce students to with the hope that they become more familiar with this language and apply it to their own learning. We hope that in providing them with the power of this language they can begin to take agency over learning and, in the process, understand themselves and their learning *better*.

If we are not aligned across grade levels within our school, students will feel confused, uncertain, and even anxious. They begin to see themselves differently depending on the teacher they're working with. In one class, they may feel confident, in control, and honoured in their learning, yet in another classroom they may feel lost, incapable, and unappreciated. *I'm not a writer* or *I'm not a math person* or *I'm not creative* are all descriptors I've heard students use when they talk about their learning or struggles in a particular classroom. They begin to see themselves in a certain way, often as a direct result of our assessment practices, assessment decisions, and assessment values.

I have worked with many students who love learning but hate assessment. They enjoy class, they enjoy their peers, they even enjoy the material they are learning about. But the moment assessment comes into play and marks, grades, and numbers enter the equation, some students disengage and disconnect from the learning.

I have seen many students stop coming to class because assessment causes such a significantly negative stress response. They believe the only way they can deal with the issue is to avoid it altogether. I am a huge proponent of self-regulated and social emotional learning, and I do believe that these skills need to be taught in schools and nurtured in our students. But in the face of an inequitable assessment practice, it is unfair for our students to work through things when we, the teachers working with these students, have created the conditions for confusion, chaos, and stress to reign.

The question remains: How can we create more of an equitable assessment practice across our school and plan for assessment alignment to ensure that all students have an equal chance of success?

To grow a culture of inquiry and create assessment equity, ensuring every stakeholder is talking about teaching and learning using similar language is critical.

To help bring this conversation to your school and your colleagues, I suggest starting small and working toward bigger changes. Discuss assessment as a staff to begin to identify where alignment exists in your assessment work and where you need to shift your beliefs and assessment practices to ensure equity and agency for all students. With this in mind, I suggest starting with the following exercise.

INTRODUCE THE VISION

Devote time to identifying the landscape of assessment and what the school, the staff, and subsequently the students will value, prioritize, and work toward. I suggest having the staff work in small faculty groups or teams. Each team of teachers will be prompted to discuss a series of guiding questions focused on creating assessment alignment and equity across the school. The teams will be asked to document their thinking so it can be shared out to other groups throughout the time spent exploring these ideas. This documentation will be displayed in a manner that provides all teachers an opportunity to step back and look for patterns, common ideas, and direction.

This process and the information teachers identify will create the foundation for alignment and equity of assessment for students in the school. Spending time reviewing what teachers shared and documented, drawing out the common beliefs and strategies, and forming ideas that will tie assessment planning together is of the utmost importance. It's critical that the key ideas and common beliefs that emerge from this discussion are at the heart of the subsequent work faculties and individual teachers will embark on.

Get started with some or all of these prompts:

- Reflect on your assessment practice; what is something you would like to let go of? What is something you would like to elevate and bring to your practice with more intentionality?
- How do you use your assessment practice to guide your planning and your time with your students? How much do you involve students in this process? How can you involve

students more in this process? How does your assessment inform your teaching, your teaching shape your assessment, and student voice elevate the entire process?

- How do you make learning goals visible to your students? How well do your students know the learning goals? If I were to sit and chat with your students about the learning goals in your classroom, what would they say? Would they speak as articulately on the topic as you would?

- Inherently, teachers are the assessment experts in the classroom, especially when it comes to feedback on learning. How can you give up some control over feedback in your practice? How can you help your students become more accurate and confident in their feedback to one another?

- How much is student voice a part of how you report to parents about student learning? How could you include more student voice in the reporting process to parents?

- How certain are you that you can communicate what successful learning looks like in your classroom? Please describe what successful learning looks like in your room.

- Often in the classroom, teachers know where each particular student is at in their learning, where they need to go next, and how they can go about getting there. How well do you know this about each of your students? Better yet, how well do each of your students know this about themselves? If I were to ask them this question, what would they say?

- How do you know there is alignment between what you hope students learn and what students actually learn?

- How are you supporting students in the process of reflecting on their learning, setting personal goals, and spending time conferring with them on these learning goals?

Ideally the information gathered from this activity and the rich discussion and sharing that ensues sets the stage for diving into this book more meaningfully as a staff and culture of learning. Rather than merely having a few teachers adopt the principles, values, behaviours, and tasks that you've read about, these guiding questions set the stage for teacher reflection, a broader thirst for assessment transformation, and the active commitment to explore the possibilities of a more student-centred assessment practice, one in which student agency and inquiry will empower learners, inform teachers, and create a culture of inquiry in your school.

Although this chapter comes toward the conclusion of this book, this activity is truly the start point for your school's assessment journey. Circle back to the beginning now and facilitate a book club or collaborative inquiry through the principles, values, behaviours, and tasks I have shared with you. Work together. Enlist the engagement and possibilities of your students in this process. Set your sights toward lofty ideals and ideas: Your students—and you—are worth it.

#INQUIRYMINDSET IN ACTION

Document this activity in a manner that will allow you to revisit it in the coming weeks and months. Whether it is using chart paper, Google Docs, Padlet, or Google Slides, capturing the discourse amongst your colleagues is critical. These artifacts will represent the start point of your assessment journey. Consider how you want this to look, what would make the most sense for your staff, what would be the most intuitive yet engaging format for you all to partake in, and what would yield an artifact you can easily save and refer to.

INQUIRY AS A RESPONSIVE PEDAGOGY: THE POWER OF THE PIVOT

As an inquiry coach and consultant, I often observe educators in lessons with students in their classrooms. I am typically invited into their space, given a lesson plan, and asked to provide feedback on what I see. It is a wonderful opportunity to watch passionate teachers do what they love. I always find joy in this experience.

Having done this countless times, I've come to understand that one of the most powerful behaviours exhibited by a teacher in inquiry is their responsiveness. Certainly, inquiry requires strong planning, intentionality, a deep understanding of our curriculum, and a clear picture of what we want for our students. This we know is true. Yet inquiry can fall short when teachers take too much control over learning and don't first harness student curiosity, interest, and passion—and plan accordingly from these. The lone skill that allows teachers to be successful in co-designing units of inquiry and having their lessons guide learners into *experiencing* the curriculum is their willingness to be responsive educators.

I call this responsiveness *the power of the pivot.*

The power of the pivot may occur when a teacher hears a student's curiosity, recognizes a wonder they have, and pivots away from their lesson plan or their perceived pathway for learning to explore this interest more meaningfully in class.

The power of the pivot may occur when a teacher has a fantastic idea—something they hope will spark student engagement and wonder—yet when they speak with students, observe their learning, and notice their wonderings and questions, they use these insights to pivot in another, perhaps unforeseen, direction.

The power of the pivot may occur when a student need surfaces and the inquiry teacher recognizes that a different approach, some intentional scaffolding, or some heartfelt TLC call on them to pivot to better meet the needs of their learners.

The power of the pivot may occur as we get to know our students better, as we build relationships with each of them, and as we learn who they are, what they believe in, and what they value. It occurs as we, ourselves, unpack our biases and understand how our own identity, beliefs, and values shape both why and how we teach.

Inquiry-based learning is a responsive, agile, nuanced, and responsive pedagogy that empowers students to take ownership over their learning.

What follows is a deep dive into this notion of responsiveness. I ask that as you read, you reflect on your own teaching. Consider just how responsive you are in working with students. Identify ways in which you embody what it means to pivot in inquiry. The memories you recall, the experiences you have lived, and the stories you can share all represent your own ability to pivot.

Let's dive in!

RESPONSIVE TO STUDENT CURIOSITIES

To explore authentic and personalized inquiry with our students, we must first grasp their curiosities.

- What do our students want to learn avbout?
- What are their interests outside of class?
- What are they reading, watching, and doing in their home lives that we can potentially explore together at school?
- How can we bring the curriculum to life for our students?
- How can we help students discover context and personal relevance in the curriculum?

As we unpack the answers to these questions, we discover how we can be more responsive to student curiosities. Let me share two brief experiences I have had that demonstrate how adults can either squelch curiosity or nurture it to grow into something special.

I visited the Art Institute of Chicago, one of the oldest and largest art museums in the United States. A magnificent building constructed in the 1880s, the institute is stunning. With more than 300,000 works of art as well as over thirty special exhibitions, the institute includes Grant Wood's *American Gothic*, Picasso's *Old Guitarist*, and an impressive Andy Warhol collection. From the moment you approach the grand stairs outside the building until you depart the Art Institute of Chicago is wondrous. Exhibits pull you in to them. You cannot help but feel a sense of awe at the interesting array of pieces and collections on display.

On the day of my visit, several school groups, mostly at the primary level, were on a field trip to the Institute. I recall thinking that what awaited these kids would certainly impress on them an interest in art and, potentially, a fondness or love that could stay with them into their adulthood. One day in their futures, they may find themselves exploring a museum in a city that isn't their own, just as I was, following a curiosity about art that began on this particular day at the Art Institute of Chicago. I remember thinking how special it was that we would share in this experience together.

As I made my way through the museum, I kept finding myself surrounded by one school group in particular. Our timing through each exhibit was similar, and I got to hear their comments as they explored the art from space to space: *oohs* and *aahs*, running feet, pointing fingers, quiet stillness, contemplative curiosity. The youngsters were clearly enjoying themselves as each student explored the contemporary cathedral-like chasms filled with art.

What occurred at one exhibit struck me, and not in a good way. It was a fascinating interactive display, a series of furniture and objects from a ski resort in the French Alps dating back to the 1960s. The collection was the work of a French architect who designed prefabricated pod-like living units during the ski culture boom of the era to be easily installed in lodges and chalets. Some of these pods had been transported to the Institute so visitors could stroll through them, touch the surfaces, and feel what life was like in those French Alp resorts more than sixty years ago. The colours, textures, smells, and sensations took the viewer back to another place in another time.

Just as they had throughout the day, the same class of youngsters soon caught up with me. As they joined me in this inviting exhibit, I eagerly anticipated seeing their response to the unique space and the interesting artifacts. As soon as they rounded the corner and their eyes caught the cool, space-like structures, they galloped toward the display. I could see their wide eyes. I could hear their fascination. I could sense their curiosity. It was palpable. The kids were literally running with awe toward the entrance to the exhibit, ready to explore, engage, and enjoy.

But just as the group approached the first pod, a gallery attendant, the sort of employee who answers questions from patrons and ensures the art is protected, stepped out from his stand-to position at the exhibit entrance and halted the students dead in their tracks. The attendant raised both of his arms, palms facing forward, and strictly called on the class to stop and calm down. "Whoa! Whoa! Whoa! *Slow down.* Be careful!" He called, coming across more as a security guard than a lover of art and creativity. The attendant instructed the students to not rush through the gallery, to not touch anything, to keep their hands in their pockets, and to quiet down so as to not disturb the other visitors.

I was dumbstruck. What a missed opportunity!

In the briefest of moments, he squelched the curiosity of the entire group. Their demeanour and energy immediately changed. I could see them wanting to reach for things in the exhibit, to touch and explore and interact, and then each time, they caught themselves, looking guiltily back toward the attendant to make sure they weren't in trouble. The teacher in me knew that their learning had shifted. What could have been an amazing experience and the Velcro for future contexts and interactions and teachable moments had been overcontrolled and suffocated.

How we respond to student engagement and curiosity is critical. What was perceived as disruptive, noisy, noncompliant, and even disrespectful behaviour was in fact a reflection of personal relevance, interest, and curiosity. We must notice this potential and pivot toward this energy.

My experience at the Art Institute of Chicago is in complete contrast to the next experience I'd like to share with you.

Recently my family joined me on a trip to Australia. I had been invited there to support schools and educators in implementing inquiry, and my family came along to explore and enjoy Australia. We set aside a day to visit the Australia Zoo, home of the "crocodile hunter," Steve Irwin. I grew up enamoured with his television show, his courageous conservation of animals, and his adventurous spirit. He is an Australian hero and a hero of mine. I recall how his tragic and untimely death made an impact on me. Now, years later, I looked forward to sharing the legacy of Steve Irwin with my sons.

To say my boys were excited would be an understatement. They love zoos, and they were keen to explore Australia's finest. As we waited in the ticket line, they vibrated with enthusiasm. Within a few minutes we were given a map, we collectively planned our course through the zoo, and we set out to explore the more than 1,000 acres of wildlife and nature.

As we rounded the first corner of the zoo, we caught sight of two zookeepers, twenty feet away from us, younger women donning official uniforms, each holding an animal in their arms. One of them cradled an adorable koala, one of the animals high on our must-see-whilst-in-Australia list. The other zookeeper had a lizard draped over her arm, its long tail hanging toward the ground. Our boys leapt into action, opening their stride to a full run toward the zookeepers and the animals. It was a strikingly similar reaction to what I witnessed at the Art Institute of Chicago. Here at the Australia Zoo, however, the response from the adults in the space was entirely different.

On spotting my children's interest and enthusiasm, the two zoo-keepers simultaneously knelt, raised a single open arm, and kindly invited my sons toward them, beckoning their curiosity with a kind gesture of their hands. Their body language said *come close, have a look, engage with us,* and *experience the animals.* They asked my sons questions: "Do you know what animals these are? Would you like to know a bit about them? Would you like to carefully touch them? Would you like to hold one? What questions do you have?" In the briefest of moments, the zookeepers recognized our son's engagement and leveraged their curiosity. Within the first twenty feet of the zoo, we all knew that our day was going to be special because our curiosities had been honoured and welcomed.

How we respond to student curiosity sets the stage for learning. It recognizes and honours relevance for everyone in our classrooms. It becomes the Velcro for learning, the context on which students will attach subsequent learning, interactions, and understandings. When we welcome curiosities and weave them into our lesson and unit design, when we have an end in mind with a starting point of student relevance and interest, our curriculum comes to life for our students.

Inquiry invites student curiosity, engagement, interest, and wonder. How we respond to student curiosity sets the stage for learning.

WHAT COULD THIS LOOK LIKE?

Each year I ask my students to fill out a simple yet powerful Google Form survey titled *What Are Your Curiosities, Interests, Passions, and Talents?* I ask my students to share some information that would allow me to both get to know them better and be responsive when it comes to exploring a more personalized inquiry with them. I like to do this as a Google Form survey so I can easily access what they share.

I ask them the following questions:

- Take a moment and consider what it is you are curious about, interested in, or passionate about. What comes to mind?
- When you were a child, what did you dream of becoming one day?
- What have you put time into improving because you love setting your mind to it?
- What do you spend your time doing outside of school?
- If you could make a living doing one thing you love, what would you be doing in ten years?
- Please share any links, images, resources, or other artifacts that would help me understand your curiosity, interest, or passion.
- Do you have a file to upload and share that would help me to better understand what you've communicated? If so, please upload it here.

Time and again, I am amazed with what students share: topics and passions such as athletics, arts, music, politics, sustainability, medicine and health care, and humanitarianism, to name just a few. The results are always diverse and fascinatingly telling of who I am working with.

Being responsive to student curiosities is about not overplanning our lessons or units until we gather enough information from our students to inform our planning and next steps. Being responsive to student curiosities is about sparking enough interest for our learners so that their voice, their wonderings, and their curiosities will directly shape what we learn about. Being responsive to student curiosities is about genuinely gathering data through informal interactions and conversations and having these data begin to shape the formal processes and learning experiences for each individual student.

BE RESPONSIVE TO STUDENT QUESTIONS

All my units of inquiry are framed by an overarching unGoogleable question. Sometimes I craft this question for all students to explore in a structured, more teacher-directed inquiry. At other times, I provide a handful of questions to allow students some choice in exploring. This is more of a controlled, and still teacher-directed, inquiry. In guided inquiry, I provide my students with a concept or big idea that will frame their inquiries. This big idea will be the heart of their own personalized questions that they each craft.

Finally, in free inquiry, students select a concept or big idea of their own, one that is housed in our curriculum or can be backwards designed to our curriculum. In free inquiry, like guided, students craft their own overarching question to explore and deepen their understanding.

As you can see, questions are foundational to the inquiry classroom. Whether it is the teacher's question or the student's question, inquiry learning begins with a question. This alone presents the greatest shift a teacher can make in adopting more of an inquiry approach in their teaching: begin learning with a question.

No matter the type of inquiry—structured, controlled, guided, or free—I always spend time with students generating their own questions about our inquiry. This often occurs after we've explored a provocation and sparked their curiosity. A powerful provocation leads to questions, and the provocations I have designed are connected to our curriculum. Therefore, the engagement, the curiosity, and the questions students have are all inherently tied to our learning objectives.

I then use these student-generated questions to guide our next steps. This tends to be our first step in research as we seek to explore and answer their own questions.

This could be done in several ways:

- Students reflect and access prior knowledge. Students may ask themselves: *What do I know about this question?*
- Students ask a friend, a parent, or adult, or a teacher what they know about the question.
- Students do some research online, exploring the question.
- Students head to the library to browse and skim a variety of potentially helpful resources on the topic of the question. Students may even sign out books.
- Students ask Siri, Alexa, or Google Home the question.

Then we share our findings and explore ways that our new understanding can guide our next steps. At this point I reflect on our curriculum and consider any vocabulary terms, jargon, or concepts that could support our thinking. This can lead to some specific teaching of content and ideas that, in turn, cycle us back to more student-generated questions.

This process allows us to investigate our curriculum, to be inquirers and explorers, to be active in our learning, and to have a voice in our next steps and direction in inquiry. Asking students what questions they have and exploring these together allows us to plan and structure our inquiry.

> Questions in learning allow students to investigate the curriculum, to be inquirers and explorers, to be active in their learning, and to have a voice in our next steps and direction in inquiry.

WHAT COULD THIS LOOK LIKE?

I often work with teams of social studies teachers to help them design guided units of inquiry that are based on an overarching concept or big idea yet provide agency for students to delve into a relevant, personal interest or curiosity. One concept we consistently use in our planning of this guided inquiry unit focuses on the concept of conflict. Rather than the traditional approach to teaching twentieth-century history, chronologically unpacking events from the start of the century to the end, in the guided-inquiry experience, students explore twentieth-century history through a conceptual lens.

Through a conceptual lens, I encourage teachers to select a single case study of conflict from their curriculum, one that allows them to spark curiosity, create engagement, and provide a clear understanding of the key concepts with the overarching big idea of conflict. The phrase *key concepts* refers to the specific unifying threads across every conflict. Key concepts are the checkpoints of a big idea, the details that allow us to make connections and merge case studies; it's the synthesis amongst concepts.

Examples of the key concepts of conflict could include any of the following:

- political, economic, or social inequalities
- extreme poverty
- economic stagnation
- poor government services
- high unemployment
- environmental degradation
- individual economic incentives
- cultural dimensions related to ethnicity or religion

These key concepts will be explored through the teacher-directed case study and used as a framework for students to explore a conflict of their choosing in their own guided inquiry. Perhaps a teacher uses the details of World War I as a case study to examine the concept of conflict and deepen understanding of the key concepts. This context would provide the beginnings of understanding conflict through a conceptual lens. Using the framework of the key concepts allows students to explore their own, personalized examination of conflict through a case study that *they* decide, such as World War II, the Cold War, the Korean War, the Vietnam War, and so on.

The concept of the teacher's choosing and a case study that is teacher directed provides students with the skills and understanding to succeed in their own inquiry as they explore their own questions that are rooted in the concept. Through modeling and exploring key concepts, students can apply this framework to answer their own questions and create their own learning path. Guided inquiry is one type of inquiry that allows teachers to be responsive to student questions.

Let me provide some meaningful context. I was once observing a history teacher co-design a guided inquiry unit of study with her students that focused on the concept of conflict. Throughout the unit of inquiry, she modeled and coached the inquiry process revolving around a conflict case study that was more teacher directed: World War II. When it came time for students to take agency over the case study and demonstrate their understanding of the concept of conflict, two different and telling responses emerged from a couple of students who shared similar cultural upbringings and family histories.

One student of Korean descent with strong ties to the culture and their family's experiences throughout the Korean War selected this conflict as their focused case study. When asked why they selected this case study, the student shared that family members had fought in this war. Some perished; others survived. The student had access to family relics to examine and refer to in research and learning. Family members who were alive during the conflict would provide firsthand accounts. Choosing this case study was highly meaningful to this student, who spoke passionately and meaningfully about personal reasons and hopes for learning.

Another student, also of Korean descent with similar strong ties to the culture and family's experiences throughout the Korean War, decided to not select this conflict to study. The student was adamant and clear that this case study was not something of personal interest. When the teacher gently asked why the student was so adamant about not choosing the Korean War as a focus, even though she possessed an authentic family connection to the conflict, she shared an entirely different and opposite set of values toward the case study from that of the previous student. Although she also had family members who fought and perished or survived the war, the conflict hit too close to home. The thought of exploring the Korean War more deeply was triggering, and the student anticipated it would surface some unwanted and unnecessary trauma for herself and her family.

By empowering our students with choice within the curriculum, we are not only centring their interests and their curiosities; we are also centring their culture. In doing so, we are decentring ourselves and our perhaps unforeseen or unrecognized biases and prejudices and truly putting students in the active role of co-designing their learning. We are lifting the cultural awareness and understanding of everyone in the room. We are presenting the curriculum and the concepts we study through the lens of exploration and discovery through a responsive process of inquiry.

By empowering our students with choice within the curriculum, we are not only centring their interests and their curiosities; we are also centring their culture.

Being responsive to student questions means not always having our own questions dictate learning. Rather, the inquiry teacher must empower student questioning to shape an inquiry that is highly personalized to each individual student. Being responsive to student questions means providing students with the skills of a strong questioner, someone who understands the difference between closed- and open-ended questions and how they both are pivotal in inquiry. Being responsive to student questions means providing the space, acceptance, and support for student questions to have a meaningful role in our classroom.

BE RESPONSIVE TO STUDENTS' NEEDS

In my opinion, educators face no greater challenge today than how well we meet the needs of such diverse and unique students. Throughout my career, it has been this lone endeavour that has guided my own professional learning and shaped how I interact with students and their families every day. Inquiry has allowed me to discover a powerful balance between what I must teach, how I can teach it, and how I can engage students to have agency over their learning.

Part of the success I have discovered, and the subsequent confidence students attain, is directly correlated to getting to know my students' needs. The challenges they face, the barriers to learning they may possess, the hesitancies they may feel, and the triggers that they may encounter all inform me of how I can help my learners have a fulfilling and meaningful experience.

Inevitably the challenge isn't in acknowledging the truth that getting to know our students allows us to better meet their needs. The challenge we face is in how we go about getting to know them better to an extent that allows us and them to *overcome* these challenges. I have spent my career sharpening my interactions with students as well as designing inquiry experiences that enable me to identify the needs of each student in the room.

One of the most powerful steps in the inquiry process is reflection. Throughout inquiry, I often call on students to consider the process of learning and identify both areas where they feel they demonstrated success and areas that they feel stretched or challenged them. Reflection provides students the opportunity to identify these critical components of their learning on their own, with the teacher facilitating the reflection process.

Teachers traditionally assess and tell students what they're good at and what they're not good at, areas of strength and areas to improve. This can be demoralizing for students and cause a distaste for assessment. They quickly become disconnected from learning and complacent in the classroom. They become accustomed to waiting for what the teacher tells them, waiting for the teacher's assessment, and waiting for the teacher's authority. In a way, their identity ceases to be theirs. Their sense of self is now in the hands of what someone else has to say about them, about how someone else sees them and assesses them.

The heartbreaking truth of traditional assessment practices is that it carries severe consequences. Students lose touch with the natural pathways by which humans learn. We observe, we plan, we attempt, we reflect, we revise, and we try again. We construct knowledge. Learning is a verb in which there's movement, action, and deep thinking. When students are not given an opportunity to reflect and have a voice in the assessment process, they lose sight of the exact skills human beings need to navigate the world beyond school.

WHAT COULD THIS LOOK LIKE?

Reflection occurs in many forms. One reflection activity I employ at the start of units of inquiry rings especially true when it comes to being responsive to students' needs.

Before undertaking a task, any collaborative work, or a unit of inquiry, I ask students to partake in a *learner inventory*. I prompt them to reflect and take stock of how they are feeling about the inquiry, what strengths they bring to learning, and what areas of our inquiry may stretch and challenge them.

I ask them the following questions:

- What are you good at?
- What can you rely on as strengths in this activity, in this step of the inquiry process, or in this type of inquiry?

- What might you need help with?
- What might you help others with?
- Who could help you in this area of need? Who could you help?
- How are you currently feeling about your learning?
- Are there any big feelings you are encountering that you'd like me to know about?

I also use the Types of Student Inquiry sketchnote to help students reflect more deeply and to support them in identifying some specific areas they'd like to highlight in their sharing. I often ask students, *as we transition from one type of inquiry to the next, which competencies do you feel have improved over time? Which competencies do you feel you might need to continue to develop? How are you feeling about taking on more agency over your learning?* I print off and post this sketchnote in my class so we can refer to it throughout learning. It is also attached to our course syllabus, allowing parents to see our learning process as well as for students to use it during this reflection activity.

Each student's self-identified strengths and challenges provide me with extremely helpful information as to how I can best meet their needs. I use their strengths by calling on students throughout learning to lean into these skills. I remind them that they can continuously revisit what they're good at and what their sharpest tools are. I remind them to find confidence and success in these areas.

I have found that we can set the stage for success by reminding students repeatedly and consistently they are capable and that they have certain skills and understandings that they've identified as strengths. These reminders help them acquire an optimistic outlook on learning, empowering them to self-regulate more consistently and demonstrate a growth mindset. Learning becomes an *I can* feeling rather than an *I can't* feeling.

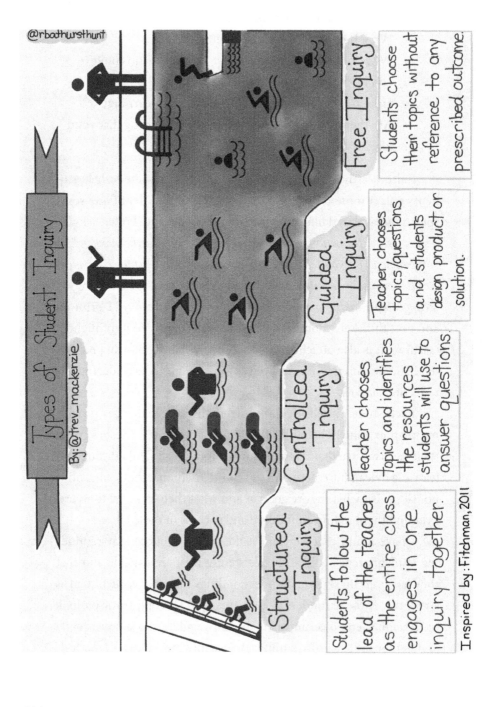

I also ask students to identify a single competency or area that they will focus on improving and working toward strengthening throughout inquiry. I ask for just a single competency, because anything more can have a countereffect on the confidence students have gained from identifying their strengths. That optimistic outlook on learning, the one founded on feeling capable and successful, is now lost underneath the feelings of not being able to achieve multiple goals they've set for themselves. Goals should be achievable and meaningful. Narrowing my student's focus to a single goal helps ensure this is the case.

All of our students have strengths. As educators, we must shift our perspective from a stance of comparing each student with one another and toward a belief that each child is capable, has potential, and can be successful. We must empower our students with the skill of reflection so we can nurture metacognition and harness agency of learning.

We record these strengths and challenges in a variety of ways. Sometimes students journal about them throughout inquiry as evidence of formative reflection and independent decision-making. Other times students document their reflections in a planning template that helps them outline the process of their inquiry and how they will rely on their strengths and identify solutions and strategies to help cope with challenges as they arise.

At times I call on students to share these reflections publicly by posting their strengths and challenges for their classmates to see. I love this activity because it builds a learning community founded on openness, trust, empathy, connectedness, and a mutual commitment to support one another in learning. I ask them to record their reflections on a sticky note and post them in the front of our class on our whiteboard to either a strengths side titled *Things I want people to know about me...my strengths* or a stretches side titled *Things I want people to know about me...my stretches.* Together we observe the board, look for trends and clusters, and discuss strategies that work for each of us with an ear to listening for strategies that we could possibly adopt as our own.

Being responsive to students' needs means helping students understand themselves better. By helping them to know their learning strengths and challenges, we can help them take appropriate action. Being responsive to students' needs means asking students to reflect on their learning, constantly observing and noticing how they are feeling and how they say they are doing. Being responsive to students' needs means providing personalized strategies for each individual student and helping them track progress in working toward meeting their own goals. Being responsive to students' needs means giving students voice in assessment through genuine decision-making and reflection.

RESPONSIVE TO STUDENT IDENTITY

No matter the age of my students or the grade level I teach, I begin every year with an inquiry into self. I have several goals for this unit, each one equally important in ensuring we have a successful and meaningful school year together.

First, I aim to model inquiry and introduce students to the shallow end of the inquiry pool. For many students, this will be their first experience in inquiry. As such, I focus on slowing down the unit and unpacking each element together as a class. Understanding the role of questions in inquiry, becoming accustomed to how we respond to provocations, and grasping their purpose in our learning allows us to launch inquiry more successfully. As we sharpen relevant and successful research skills and explore student curiosities and interests, we can have these shape our unit design and learning intentions.

The first structured unit sets the stage for the rest of the year and how we will explore the different types of student inquiry. As student agency shifts and learners increasingly experience how their voice and their ideas will directly shape their learning, it is this first unit and the modeling I facilitate that will ensure they are confident and successful later in the year.

Second, I want to get to know my students better. I want them to openly share their curiosities, interests, goals, and passions in class. I want to have their identity shape our learning and frame my unit planning. I want to know what they value, what they believe in, and how they view the world. I want to create powerful relationships with each student. I want our time together to be built on trust—a trust that will allow us to explore our vulnerabilities, take risks, and support one another throughout the process. I want the learning to be personally meaningful and fulfilling to every student in the room. An inquiry into self allows us to have the type of discussions that permit me to get to know all of these aspects of the learners with whom I am working.

And finally, I want my students to get to know *themselves* better. I want them to grasp that our classroom will be a space that values who they are and who they want to become. I want them to reflect on their learning and identify their strengths as well as their stretches. I want them to share their values and convictions. I want them to understand their biases and prejudices. I want them to grasp the countless ways in which our society shapes us, how our culture impacts us, and how, without us even knowing it, our sense of self is shaped by many factors that we have absolutely no control over. I want them to experience genuine agency over learning, and in the process, build confidence in the classroom and leave our time together with a love for learning that perhaps they haven't felt in a long time.

I want students to experience genuine agency over learning, and in the process build confidence in the classroom and leave our time together with a love for learning that perhaps they haven't felt in a long time.

WHAT COULD THIS LOOK LIKE?

The overarching unGoogleable question we explore together that frames this structured inquiry into self is *Who are you and what shapes your identity?* (See the Learner Identity questions in Chapter 6, "Asking the Right Questions" on page 83.) Although seemingly broad and unspecific, this question provides a certain scope and depth for each individual student to explore themselves in a highly personalized manner.

I post this question in a highly visible space in our classroom, typically above our projector screen. This allows us to all see the question throughout our learning and refer to it as we share insights, unpack resources, make connections, and build on our thinking. It is this question that will shape the resources we unpack, guide our discussions, shape our learning, and provide the direction for our inquiry.

Once the question is posted, we discuss our thoughts and share our reactions to the question. We access prior knowledge, we document our thinking, and we compose our initial beliefs. I want students to have some evidence of their thinking at the start of an inquiry so we can reflect on this evidence later in the process of learning after we've done some research and constructed new understandings. I want to explore with them whether their thinking changed and what they experienced, read, or learned more about that caused this shift.

At this point in the inquiry, I enjoy modeling my unpacking of my own identity in a write-aloud activity. I love write-alouds. I simply stand at the whiteboard and write to the prompt I plan on giving students, putting words to my thoughts as I write, making the occasional mistake as I go, modeling my thinking and planning, all the while inviting them in to understand me better. I learned this strategy from a good educator friend and author I deeply admire named Adrienne Gear. Adrienne shares with us some insight on the process of bringing write-alouds to your classroom. Have a read:

> *I often wonder what it would be like to sit beside my favorite writer (I have many!) while they are in the depths of writing their next novel or picture book. Not only to observe them writing, but to somehow crawl inside their head and listen to their inside voice as they transform thought into words. To watch this magical process as it unfolds would be a remarkable experience.*
>
> *But most writers write in silence, immersed in thought, molding words like playdough, creating visual images through word choice and sensory details. But what if we could give our students a glimpse into our thoughts as we write?*
>
> *Writing aloud, or modeled writing, is a strategy whereby teachers use a "think-aloud" strategy to share their thinking as they compose a piece of writing in front of students, helping make the writing process more visible and tangible. While the topic of the writing piece can vary, the important point is that the teacher makes his or her thought process visible to students as they proceed through the writing process. In this way, the teacher is able to explicitly demonstrate the writing process*

and directly teach key writing skills and concepts within the context of their own writing.

Cunningham and Allington believe that teacher modeling is the critical factor in student writing success. Just as reading aloud, shared reading, and guided reading strategies are essential components of an effective reading program, writing aloud helps developing writers' move toward independence. While writing aloud is seen as a scaffolded approach when teaching beginning writers, it is also an effective strategy for older writers. Regie Routman states, "Writing aloud is a powerful modeling technique at any grade level for getting students' attention and demonstrating various aspects of writing."

Using this "write-aloud" strategy provides many benefits for our developing writers. So many teachable moments are magnified when you write aloud. When students see us talking through our composition, making mistakes, editing as we go, pausing and reflecting on our word choices, talking through our writing as we write, it's like a window into our writing process.

Now "writing aloud" has its challenges. On more than one occasion, I have started a "write aloud" and realized, in the moment when all eyes and ears were on me, that my writing was gibberish nonsense! When doing a write-aloud, it helps to have done a little preparation. That does not mean writing something out and then copying it, word for word, in front of the students. There needs to be some degree of spontaneous composition occurring, but it helps to at least know the target writing technique you are aiming to model ahead of time.

Using the prompt *Who am I?*, I begin writing and speaking about my identity as I slowly unpack the layers that make me who I am. I reveal certain things about myself that students didn't know, some details that share some of my values as an educator, and some ideas that demonstrate the honesty, vulnerability, and self-analysis that I hope students will embody when they partake in their own reflection writing to the same prompt. I write to the notion of inter- sectionality and my cognizant efforts to understand all the things in life that shape my biases, prejudices, and privilege, regardless of whether I am aware of them.

It is a powerful exercise.

I then call on students to do the same but quietly and introspec- tively on their own pages (not as a write-aloud). I encourage them to be open, honest, and vulnerable in their writing and to honour the safety of their reflection and that their writing won't be shared openly. I propose that they can trust the pen on the page. As they write, students begin to unpack their own identity, the impact of cul- ture on their sense of self, and the forces that have shaped who they are, what they value, and what they believe in.

I may then introduce a series of provocations to spark curiosity and engage their interests further. I want these provocations to get my students thinking more deeply about their identity and the many factors that shape who we are and what we believe. I want to expand their thinking and stretch their understanding of self.

One provocation I introduce is an article about the science of social networks and how we are influenced by the people around us whether we know it or not. David Burkus explores this idea in his book *Friend of a Friend: Understanding the Hidden Networks That Can Transform Your Life and Career.* Burkus shares some of the research around the influence of others on our values, our beliefs, and our outlook on life. For those of you who believe we have com- plete control over our futures, Burkus's research will stretch your thinking, which is precisely what I hope my students experience when exploring this provocation.

I follow up with another provocation, this time a compelling image that forces us to consider the role that advertising, marketing, pop culture, and the media have on our sense of self. I ask students to share what they notice, what they wonder, and what they know. I challenge them to identify times when they've been aware that something or someone was trying to manipulate them to buy something, behave a certain way, or believe a particular value or principle. Their sharing is always honest and illuminating. Slowly their focus on self and their understanding of the factors that shape each of our identities is broadened. Have a look at the image provocation now.

Consumer's Mind by Christopher Dombres

I appreciate the opportunity for students to formulate their thoughts through the provocations I present. The questions they pose, the prior knowledge they possess, and the directions our learning takes us all stem from the provocation. The decision of which provocation I use is determined by whether it can spark curiosity and engagement.

Making this our initial inquiry together allows us to begin learning from a space where we have gotten to know each other better and also have gotten to know ourselves better. As we unpack identity at the start of our learning journey, I am sure to share that this is a continuous process and that together we will be reflective throughout our time together, we will be critical and inquisitive, and we will question how our learning is shaped by the curriculum and how we can shape our curriculum.

Being responsive to student identity means grounding our time together in me getting to know them and them getting to know themselves. Being responsive to student identity means honouring every student as unique beings with their own narratives, experiences, characteristics, and cultures. Being responsive to student identity means leveling the playing field of our curriculum so all students, no matter their upbringing or background, have an equitable and engaging entry point into learning. Being responsive to student identity means leveraging their prior knowledge, experiences, and narratives and providing them with the opportunity to connect these to the curriculum. Being responsive to student identity means unpacking my own biases, prejudices, and privileges openly and honestly to model the vulnerability and courage to decentre myself to centre others.

#INQUIRYMINDSET IN ACTION

At the onset of this chapter, I asked you to reflect on your own teaching as you read. I asked you to consider just how responsive you are in working with students and in what ways you pivot in inquiry. What memories came to mind? What experiences have you lived? What stories can you share that represent your own ability to pivot? Did it have to do with responding to student curiosities? Student questions? Student needs? Student identity? Or a combination of these? How can you be more responsive in your inquiry practice?

TEACHING TRANSPARENTLY: SHARING YOUR VALUES

Throughout this book, I have shared with you a series of behaviours, tasks, routines, and protocols that, over time, create the conditions for students to take on more agency over their learning and assessment. These behaviours, tasks, routines, and protocols are rooted in the values I hold dear to my practice, a series of values that manifest themselves in the day-to-day happenings of the classroom. I call these my *core values*.

I have found that incredible comfort, calm, ease, and confidence arise from students when they experience full transparency in the classroom. The Types of Student Inquiry, for example, provides a clear outline of the scaffolding of agency, that over time students will experience a gradual shift of control over learning from the teacher to the student. Throughout our time together, students will acquire the skills and understandings needed to be successful in taking on more agency over learning.

This transparency is helpful for students as we embark on a perhaps new and unfamiliar learning journey together. With this in mind, I share my core values with students at the onset of our time together. I share with them what I believe in as an educator and what goals I have for our learning community. I ask students to help keep me accountable to these values, because teaching can be a difficult and demanding job. I want them to let me know if I ever stray from these values.

I ask them to join me in making these values a central part of how we spend time together. I invite them to engage in these values and to embrace them every day. I encourage them to explore their own values as a learner and how, together, we will aim to discover our individual strengths and stretches so that we can begin to bring these skills to any context or future endeavour.

I'd like to share these values with you now just as I would with my students.

I value constructivism and the belief that each student who enters our classroom is full of rich history, experience, narrative, and understanding. I aim to lean into this prior knowledge and use it to create new understanding together. Kids do not enter our classrooms as empty vessels ready to be filled up with the content of our curriculum. We make connections. We explore our curiosities. We collaborate and co-construct.

I value competencies, dispositions, and habits of mind and the belief that the legacy of a child's schooling should be the skills and mindsets that can be applied to all of life's experiences. I value competencies such as creativity, critical thinking, collaboration, communication, curiosity, empathy, and self-control. We talk about these competencies, we set personalized goals for them, we reflect on and assess our growth toward adopting them more meaningfully, and I coach and model each of them as we observe them surfacing in class.

I value talking and thinking, and I believe that whoever is doing the talking is doing the learning. I encourage students to talk as much as possible. I have adopted equitable talk frameworks so students all have a fair opportunity to process their thoughts, rehearse their sharing, and engage in class discourse in a safe and confident manner. I share with students that the more they talk, the more effective I can be in working with them. I tell them that when they talk, I listen. I *really* listen. I want to get a better understanding of how I can support each one of them. Their talk guides my next steps.

I value wellness and ensuring that we all strive to feel good about ourselves and confident in our learning, and that we discover processes to maintain balance and well-being. I will be flexible and agile and considerate of their wellness. I will ask them how they are doing. I will call on them to reflect on their stress or anxiety, and I promise them that I will listen to their needs. I will employ structures and processes that allow students to be successful in school without jeopardizing their well-being, heightening their stress, or triggering their anxiety.

I value relationships and building a community of learning. My desire is to create a culture where trust and psychological safety allow students to take risks, be comfortable trying on new things, feel confident in giving and accepting feedback, and overall take on more ownership and agency of their learning.

I value getting to know students and, in turn, having them get to know me. I value centring students and, in turn, decentring myself. I value shifting roles in the classroom because we are partners in learning, as we co-design and co-construct, and as we collaborate and communicate.

I value agency and ensuring that students can be successful in taking on more of the heavy lifting of learning. I value partnering with students as we co-design and co-construct what learning will look like. This partnership creates equity as we centre the student and decentre ourselves. I value the behaviours, tasks, routines, and protocols that allow students to feel more comfortable, confident, and prepared to take on more responsibility over learning. I value seeing what they do with this agency and being responsive to continually get better at meeting their needs as they grow throughout our time together.

This final value takes my conversation with students to another place that focuses on exploring what we mean when we talk about *student agency*. Student agency has several facets that create a rich and fulfilling schooling experience for our students. Student agency is not merely one or two of these facets, but a collective that is nurtured through co-designing and co-constructing learning. These facets are outlined in the Learner Agency is Out of This World sketchnote. As you will see, these facets are evident throughout this book in each of the 10 Steps to Nurture Student Ownership Over Assessment.

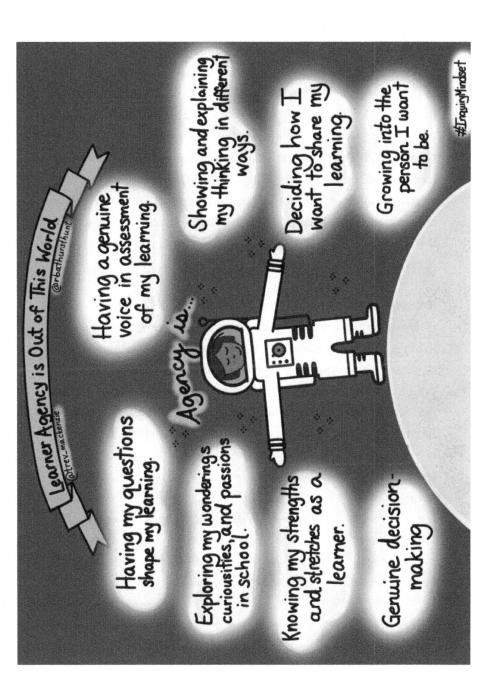

Genuine Decision-Making

Student agency is about having students take on some of the heavy lifting of learning. When students can have a genuine role in the decision-making process, this will create a classroom culture that values learning as an action. The guiding question from the Introduction was *Am I doing something my students could be doing themselves?* If the answer is yes, I decentre myself so students can take on these responsibilities. The more I do this, the more comfortable and confident they become in taking on this agency over their learning. Learning becomes a partnership between the teacher and the student as we co-design and co-construct the learning experiences together in the classroom.

Knowing My Strengths and Stretches as a Learner

I regularly ask myself whether my students know where they are at in their learning, know where they need to go next, and whether they can identify the steps they need to take to get there. Teachers can often answer these questions about their students, but can the students answer these questions for themselves? To help get these conversations started in class, I ask a series of guiding questions to help students reflect and begin to get to know themselves better as learners: *Do you learn best alone, in a small group, or in a large class setting? Do you prefer to write, talk about, or draw your learning for others to see? What is your focus threshold, as in, how long can you remain focused on something before you feel you need a change of pace, setting, or action?* These questions all help students begin to take on more ownership of their learning.

Exploring My Wonderings, Curiosities, and Passions in School

All students enter their schooling as curious and inquisitive beings. They are full of questions and wonder as they explore and discover the world around them. Somewhere in their schooling, however, many become complacent, disengaged, and uninterested in their learning and in school. What does our teaching do to support and honour the innate curiosity of all students? How do we lean into student wonderings to make rich connections to our curriculum? How can we make our curriculum come alive so students see it as something we explore and discover rather than something we merely cover? These questions help honour the wonderings, curiosities, and passions of all of our students so that they can see themselves as important stakeholders in their learning.

Having My Questions Shape My Learning

Questions are an invitation to learning. They call for us to be engaged, to be inquisitive, and to research and problem solve. Chapter 6, "Asking the Right Questions," outlines many ways that this can be honoured. Ensuring that students are becoming more competent questioners demands that we coach and model questioning in learning. Over time, students not only will begin to feel confidence in having their questions shape their learning, but their questions will be fuller, more rigorous, and worthier of exploring in the classroom.

Having a Genuine Voice in Assessment of My Learning

If we are talking about student agency in the classroom, we must ensure there is student voice in the assessment of learning as well. Students have a genuine voice in the assessment of their learning when they can confidently give accurate feedback to peers, take and apply feedback without worry of ridicule or embarrassment, and embark into learning through the lens of taking risks to grow rather than for a grade, mark, or percentage score. Students need to feel psychologically safe if we are to ask them to take on a more active and meaningful role in their learning, which is why as we nurture student agency in our classrooms, it's important that we also nurture relationships, trust, and risk-taking.

Showing and Exploring My Learning in Different Ways

Whatever the big idea or content we are learning about, I often begin the school year with a new group of students by providing a choice board for kids to explore content through. A choice board is a digital slide that I have embedded resources into that allows students some options to select information in a means that they feel best supports their learning. I often introduce the exploratory nature of a choice board by asking students, "Do you enjoy taking in information by reading text; looking at images, infographics, or charts; watching a short video; exploring a website; or listening to a podcast or someone talking about the information?" Once students have reflected on this prompt, they have a clearer understanding of what best supports their learning. When facing the options on a choice board, they decide based on their better understanding of their learning needs and strengths.

Deciding How I Want to Share My Learning

As shared in Chapter 3, "Co-Design and Co-Construct," having students reflect on their strengths and stretches and planning from these findings provides them with the opportunity to enter learning from a strength-based perspective, one of confidence, fulfillment, and personal meaning. Feelings of uncertainty, stress, and anxiety don't rear their ugly heads. Students value being given the opportunity to reflect and consider what they're good at, and how these strengths will be leveraged throughout our time together.

Growing into the Person I Want to Be

What are the enduring skills, lasting values, and habits of mind that will be the legacy of our time with children in our classrooms? How are we cultivating the conditions in today's classrooms that will nurture the empathy and equity we hope students embody as citizens of tomorrow's world? How do we view each of our students as unique individuals with strengths, talents, characteristics, and perspectives that we need to honour and help flourish during their time in school? Our active exploration of these questions and our validation of them in our interactions with students will give space and support for them to grow in our classrooms. Student agency is not about pushing all kids down the same pathway or having all kids choose the same goal. Student agency is about empowering students to know themselves better so they can determine who they want to be and identify steps toward making this goal a reality.

#INQUIRYMINDSET IN ACTION

In sharing my core values as an educator, I now ask you to reflect on your own. What drives your practice and grounds you in your teaching? What do you believe in? How do these values guide your planning, your instruction, your interactions with students, and their learning experience? How can you make these values more transparent for your students?

Additionally, please consider which of the facets of student agency you currently cultivate in your time with students. How are these facets planned for? How aware are your students that this growth and responsibility over learning is occurring? How can you bring more transparency, clarity, and direction to this process for students?

CONCLUSION

At the onset of this book, I shared with you a question that guides my teaching and informs the decisions I make in the classroom: *Am I doing something for my students that they should be doing for themselves?* I call on you to keep this guiding question with you and make it yours as you support your students in taking on more agency over their learning. I now add the following questions for you to consider:

- How are you making learning equitable for all of your students?
- How are you being responsive to the unique needs and interests and identities of everyone in your classroom?
- How are you creating space in the curriculum for students to co-design and co-construct with you?
- How is your classroom an invitation to learning? How is it a space for students to explore and discover the curriculum and in doing so, explore and discover themselves and the world around them?

- Let the guiding principles outlined in the Introduction direct you to nurture an accurate and powerful assessment compass with your students.
- Let's break down the comparison culture of assessment.
- Let's infuse more student voice in assessment.
- Let's be brave in letting go of some of our beliefs around teaching and learning.

In working toward these principles, you are on your way to making assessment something that is done inside the classroom *with* the students. Remember: Those who are doing the assessing are doing the learning. Your students will have a strong understanding of where they are, where they need to go next, and what they need to do to get there. They will have ownership over their learning and their personal growth in their schooling. Your students will have a clear understanding of success criteria, assessment tools, learning objectives, and goals. There will be frequent opportunities to reflect and confer in the *experience* of inquiry as well as in the *assessments* in inquiry. Your students will feel confident. They will have authentic ownership over their learning. They will experience an increased sense of meaning and fulfillment.

Your learning certainly doesn't end as your reading of this book comes to a close. Your ongoing exploration of these questions in your practice, your commitment to better meeting the needs of your students, and your embodiment of the Inquiry Mindset spurs you on. Your questions shape your learning. Your experiences dictate your next steps. I look forward to continuing to inquire with you.

Warmly,

Trevor

SUGGESTED READING

Guy Claxton

- *The Learning Power Approach: Teaching Learners to Teach Themselves*
- *Powering Up Your School: The Learning Power Approach to School Leadership*
- *Powering Up Students: The Learning Power Approach to High School Teaching*
- *Powering Up Children: The Learning Power Approach to Primary Teaching*
    (all titles published by Crown House Publishing)

Art Costa and Bena Kallick

- *Learning and Leading with Habits of Mind: 16 Essential Characteristics for Success* (ASCD)

Lynn Erickson

- *Transitioning to Concept-Based Curriculum and Instruction: How to Bring Content and Process Together* (Corwin)

Adrienne Gear

- *Powerful Writing Structures: Brain Pocket Strategies to Support a Year-Long Writing Program*
- *Powerful Understanding: Helping Students Explore, Question and Transform Their Thinking About Themselves, Others and the World*
    (all titles published by Pembroke Publishers)

David Gleason

- *At What Cost: Defending Adolescent Development in Fiercely Competitive Schools* (Developmental Empathy LLC)
- *Bena Kallick and Allison Zmuda*
- *Students at the Center: Personalized Learning with Habits of Mind* (ASCD)

Jay McTighe and Grant Wiggins

- *Essential Questions: Opening Doors to Student Understanding* (ASCD)

Kimberly Mitchell

- *Experience Inquiry: 5 Powerful Strategies, 50 Practical Experiences* (Corwin)

Kath Murdoch

- *The Power of Inquiry: teaching and learning with curiosity, creativity and purpose. in the contemporary classroom* (Seastar Education Consulting)

James Nottingham

- *Challenging Mindset: Why a Growth Mindset Makes a Difference in Learning—and What to Do When It Doesn't*
- *Challenging Learning through Feedback: How to Get the Type, Tone and Quality of Feedback Right Every Time* (both titles published by Corwin)

Ron Ritchhart

- *The Power of Making Thinking Visible: Practices to Engage and Empower All Learners*

- *Making Thinking Visible: How to Promote Engagement, Understanding, and Independence for All Learners*
- *Creating Cultures of Thinking: The 8 Forces We Must Master to Truly Transform Our Schools*
  (all titles published by Jossey-Bass)

Dan Rothstein and Luz Santana

- *Make Just One Change: Teach Students to Ask Their Own Questions* (Harvard Education Press)

Alexis Wiggins

- *The Best Class You Never Taught: How Spider Web Discussion Can Turn Students into Learning Leaders* (ASCD)

Dylan Wiliam

- *Embedded Formative Assessment* (National Educational Service)

ACKNOWLEDGEMENTS

My heartfelt thanks to all of the students I have supported in inquiry over the course of my career. Thank you for embracing the values of agency and the tenets of constructivism. Thank you for sharing your learning with me and allowing me to learn from you. Thank you for your bravery and leadership as we charted new and unfamiliar learning landscapes together.

Thank you to the teachers around the world who have invited me into their schools, their classrooms, and their teaching practice. All of you have personified the notion of teaching being just that, a practice. We reflect. We honour the tension, yet we lean into the softness. We find calm and ease. We collaborate and tinker together. We push one another's thinking to best meet the needs of our students. In working together, we work on ourselves.

Thank you to my critical friends and the school of thinking I now call home: Kath Murdoch; Kimberly Mitchell; Ron Ritchhart; Guy Claxton; Dan Rothstein; Jay McTighe; Art Costa; Bena Kallick; Allison Zmuda; Alexis Wiggins; Adrienne Gear; James Nottingham. The list goes on. I am truly standing on the shoulders of giants. Your guidance, passion, expertise, and commitment fill my inquiry heart.

A special thanks to a good lad: Will Moore. Your kind support of my growth, your asking and your listening, your showing a genuine interest in my interests, and the many trails we have walked together all have lent to this book coming into existence. The next jar is on me.

—

REFERENCES

Burkus, David. *Friend of a Friend ...: Understanding the Hidden Networks That Can Transform Your Life and Your Career.* Boston: Houghton Mifflin Harcourt, 2018.

Brookhart, S., Chappuis, J., Hattie, J., Johnston, P., Tovani, C., Wiggins, G., William, D. *Educational Leadership.* ASCD, 2012. Feedback for Learning. Volume 70, Number 1.

Cunningham, Patricia M, and Richard L. Allington.Classrooms That Work: They Can All Read and Write. Boston: Allyn and Bacon, 1999.

Dombres, Christopher. "Consumer's Mind." flickr.com/photos/christopherdombres/4507954714. 2008,

Duckworth, Angela. "Grit: the power of passion and perseverance." TED Talk. (May 9, 2013). youtu.be/H14bBuluwB8.

Gear, Adrienne. *Powerful Writing Structures: Brain Pocket Strategies to Support a Year-Long Writing Program.* Pembroke Publishers, 2020.

MacKenzie, T. [@tntmackenzie]. *Inquiry Live with Ron Ritchhart* [IGTV]. Instagram. instgram.com/tntmackenzie. (2020, August 27).

Ritchhart, Ron. *The Power of Making Thinking Visible: Practices to Engage and Empower All Learners.* Jossey-Bass, 2020.

Routman, Regie, and Regie Routman.Invitations: Changing as Teachers and Learners, K–12. Portsmouth, NH: Heinemann, 1994.

Wiggins, Alexis. *The Best Class You Never Taught: How Spider Web Discussion Can Turn Students into Learning Leaders.* ASCD, 2017.

Wiliam, Dylan. *Embedded Formative Assessment.* National Educational Service, 2011.

ARE YOU READY TO ELEVATE YOUR INQUIRY MINDSET?

1. **Host a Workshop at Your School**

   - Inquiry Mindset Workshop—Create and Customize Learning for Your Classroom (a one-day event)
   - Engage Me! Learn How to Transition into the Inquiry Classroom (a half-day event)
   - Private Label—The authors will customize an online or face-to-face workshop to fit your school's needs.

2. **Expert in Residence**

   - Plan a partnership with Trevor that builds capacity in an ongoing manner as the learning (and the relationship) spans across an extended period of time.

3. **Take the Online Course**

   - An online Inquiry Mindset series that is collaboratively designed for your context
   - Stay tuned to Trevor's website for ongoing online learning opportunities where teachers from around the world learn in inquiry together

4. **Schedule Trevor for a Keynote: A Different Kind of Learning: Stories from the Inquiry Classroom**

    - Have Trevor set an inspiring course for your staff or event through sharing stories from the inquiry classroom, stories of student leadership and agency over learning, stories of doing schooling differently to truly change education, and stories of relationship, where kindness and humour break down walls, allowing students to meaningfully engage, achieve, and impact.

    - Be prepared for a heartfelt and passionate keynote experience that is certain to leave you full of wonder, vision, and excitement to adopt a different kind of learning as your own!

For more information or to request a workshop, visit:

🌐 trevormackenzie.com

✉️ trevormackenzie.com/contact

🐦 @trev_mackenzie

📷 @tntmackenzie

ABOUT THE AUTHOR

TREVOR MACKENZIE is an experienced teacher, author, keynote speaker, and inquiry consultant who has worked in schools around the world, including Australia, Asia, North America, South Africa, and Europe. Trevor's passion is in supporting schools in implementing inquiry-based learning practices. He is a highly regarded speaker known for his heartfelt storytelling, kind demeanour, informed practice, and student-first philosophy.

Trevor's graduate research focused on identifying and removing the barriers to implementing inquiry-based learning in the K–12 setting. He is an inquiry practitioner currently as a teacher with the Greater Victoria School District in Victoria, Canada. He has two previous publications: *Dive into Inquiry: Amplify Learning and Empower Student Voice* and *Inquiry Mindset: Nurturing the Dreams, Wonders, & Curiosities of Our Youngest Learners*, both published by Elevate Books Edu. He has vast experience supporting schools across several years in implementation strategies in public schools, international schools, and International Baccalaureate programmes (PYP/MYP/DP).

Connect with Trevor

- trevormackenzie.com
- trevormackenzie.com/contact
- @trev_mackenzie
- @tntmackenzie

Made in the USA
Monee, IL
19 May 2021